TRADITIONAL
PUB GRUB

TRADITIONAL PUB GRUB

recipes for classic British food

RYLAND PETERS & SMALL

LONDON • NEW YORK

First published (as *Easy British Cooking*) in the United Kingdom in 2007.
This edition published in 2017 by
Ryland Peters & Small
20–21 Jockey's Fields
London WC1R 4BW

www.rylandpeters.com

10 9 8 7 6 5 4 3 2 1

Designer Jo Fernandes
Editor Céline Hughes
Picture Research Emily Westlake
Production Gordana Simakovic
Publishing Director Alison Starling

Indexer Sandra Shotter

Notes:
All spoon measurements are level unless otherwise specified.

Uncooked or partly cooked eggs should not be served to the very young, the very old or frail, or to pregnant women.

Testing for set in jam-making:
Before you start making jam, always put a saucer and 2–3 teaspoons in the refrigerator to cool. Boil the reduced preserve hard for 5 minutes, then take the pan off the heat and test for set. Take a teaspoon of the preserve, put it on the cold saucer in the refrigerator or freezer and leave for 5 minutes. Push it with a finger – if it offers resistance or crinkles, it is ready.

To sterilize preserving jars, wash them in hot, soapy water and rinse in boiling water. Place in a large pan, then cover with hot water. With the saucepan lid on, bring the water to the boil and continue boiling for 15 minutes. Turn off the heat, then leave the jars in the hot water until just before they are to be filled. Sterilize the lids for 5 minutes, by boiling, or according to the manufacturer's instructions. Jars should be filled and sealed while they are still hot.

contents

introduction

The British Isles have never been blessed with fine weather but if there's been one positive thing to come out of this, it is the natural British gift for cooking the best comfort food. When the dark evenings loom and it's blowing a gale outside, we Brits know how to rustle up a warming casserole, a life-affirming pie or a mouth-watering crumble to make us glad to be in out of the cold.

Years of humble dishes cobbled together from leftovers and storecupboard essentials, and designed to satisfy a big appetite have brought us time-honoured favourites, such as Lancashire hotpot, toad-in-the-hole, cottage pie and steak and kidney pudding. All these, alongside classic trifle, lemon curd, syllabub and bread and butter pudding, are coming to the fore again and becoming popular dishes in gastropubs and homes around the country.

Traditional Pub Grub brings you all these and plenty more British-inspired gems. The recipes here will encourage you to make the most of seasonal produce – to celebrate summer with a berry-packed summer pudding and see in the autumn with blackberry cranachan. There is also much to learn about the myriad regional dishes on offer – Scottish shortbread, Welsh speckled teabread, Irish soda bread, and Yorkshire cheesecake, to name but a few.

Finally, if there's one occasion that epitomizes the British culinary tradition, it's the inimitable afternoon tea. With a whole chapter dedicated to this noble tradition, your British cooking repertoire will be complete.

Dip into this indipensable book and discover what easy, hearty and delicious recipes British cooking has to offer.

soups, starters and snacks

Watercress has fresh crunch and a subtle peppery taste – a real palate cleanser. Buy it in bunches, with long stems, an abundance of flawless dark green leaves and a clean fresh smell. Store in the refrigerator, wrapped in damp newspaper or kitchen paper, for up to 2 days.

2 tablespoons olive oil

1 onion, chopped

1 leek, chopped

2 large potatoes, chopped

2 teaspoons plain flour

1.2 litres chicken or
vegetable stock

300 g watercress, stalks removed
and leaves chopped

a bunch of fresh flat leaf
parsley, chopped

sea salt and freshly ground
black pepper

serves 8

watercress soup

Heat the olive oil in a large saucepan and add the onion, leek and potatoes. Cook for 15 minutes, or until soft and translucent.

Add the flour, mix well, then add the stock and a little seasoning. Heat to simmering and cook for 30 minutes. Using a handheld blender, process until smooth.

Add the watercress and parsley and simmer for 5 minutes. Season to taste, then serve.

This is a gorgeously smooth and velvety soup that will suit all tastes and any occasion, from picnics to dinner parties. To ensure a really smooth texture, it is very important to blend, then sieve the soup before serving hot or chilled.

leek and potato soup
with watercress purée

75 g unsalted butter

2 onions, finely chopped

500 g leeks (white part only), finely chopped

175 g floury potatoes, chopped

1.35 litres chicken stock

300 ml milk

150 ml crème fraîche, plus extra to serve

sea salt and freshly ground white pepper

watercress purée

125 g watercress, stalks removed

5 tablespoons extra virgin olive oil

serves 6

To make the watercress purée, put the watercress leaves in a blender with the olive oil. Blend until smooth. Pour into a screwtop jar and set aside until needed.

To make the soup, melt the butter in a large saucepan and add the onions and leeks. Stir well, add 3 tablespoons water, cover tightly and cook over gentle heat for 10 minutes, or until soft and golden, but not at all brown.

Stir in the potatoes and chicken stock. Bring to the boil, reduce the heat, cover and simmer for 20 minutes, or until the potatoes are tender. Stir in the milk, then purée in a blender or with a handheld blender. Press the purée through a sieve, then return it to the pan. Stir in the crème fraîche and season. Leave to cool and chill (if serving chilled, add extra seasoning) or serve hot in warm soup bowls with a swirl of watercress purée and dollop of chilled crème fraîche.

A few dried porcini will give a stronger flavour to a soup made with regular cultivated mushrooms. Use large portobellos to give a deeper colour as well as flavour.

cream of mushroom soup

25 g dried porcini mushrooms

4 tablespoons olive oil

6 large portobello mushrooms, wiped, trimmed and sliced

1 onion, finely chopped

3 garlic cloves, peeled and crushed

a pinch of freshly grated nutmeg

leaves from a large bunch of fresh parsley, finely chopped

1.25 litres boiling chicken or vegetable stock

4 tablespoons butter

4 tablespoons plain flour

sea salt and freshly ground black pepper

to serve

4–6 tablespoons coarsely chopped fresh parsley

4–6 tablespoons crème fraîche

serves 4–6

Put the dried porcini in a bowl, add 250 ml boiling water and let soak for at least 15 minutes. Heat the olive oil in a frying pan, add the portobello mushrooms and sauté until coloured but still firm. Reserve a few slices.

Add the onion to the frying pan and sauté until softened, then add the garlic, nutmeg and parsley. Rinse any grit out of the porcini and strain their soaking liquid several times through muslin or a tea strainer. Add the liquid and the porcini to the pan. Bring to the boil, then transfer to a food processor. Add 2 ladles of the boiling stock, then pulse until creamy but still chunky.

Heat the butter in a saucepan, stir in the flour and cook gently, stirring constantly, until the mixture is very dark brown (take care or it will burn). Add the remaining stock, 1 ladle at a time, stirring well after each addition. Add the mushroom mixture, bring to the boil, then simmer for 20 minutes. Season to taste, then serve topped with the reserved mushrooms, parsley and a spoonful of crème fraîche.

note If you use a blender to make soup, the purée will be very smooth. If you use a food processor, it will be less smooth, and if you use the pulse button, you can make the mixture quite chunky.

One of the great classics of the soup world is pea and ham soup – a comforting, warming winter soup. This is a modern version using fresh or frozen peas and readily available bacon.

fresh pea soup
with mint and crispy bacon

1 tablespoon olive oil

4–8 slices very thinly cut smoked streaky bacon

500 g shelled peas, fresh or frozen

1 litre boiling ham or chicken stock, or water

sea salt and freshly ground black pepper

4 tablespoons single cream, to serve

serves 4

Heat the olive oil in a frying pan, add the bacon and sauté until crisp. Remove and drain on crumpled kitchen paper, or drape over a wooden spoon so it curls.

To cook the peas, microwave on HIGH for 3–4 minutes, or follow the package instructions. Alternatively, simmer in boiling water with a pinch of salt for 2–3 minutes or until tender. Drain.

Put the peas in a blender with 1–2 ladles of the boiling stock. Blend to a purée, adding extra stock if necessary. Add the remaining stock and blend again. Taste and adjust the seasoning. Reheat, thinning with a little boiling water if necessary, then ladle into heated soup bowls and serve, topped with the crispy bacon and a swirl of cream.

variation Cook the peas, drain and leave to cool, then put in the blender with 8 ice cubes and enough water to make the blades run. Blend to a purée, then thin with iced water to the consistency you like. Season to taste and serve topped with sliced spring onions.

Welsh rabbit – also known as rarebit – is a glorified version of cheese on toast. It dates back to the mid-sixteenth century, but over time has evolved into countless variations. If you fancy a comforting snack, this easy-to-make version is hard to beat.

welsh rabbit

25 g butter

1 onion or 4 shallots, sliced

100 g Cheddar, grated

75 ml ale or lager

1 teaspoon mustard

a pinch of sea salt

2 eggs, lightly beaten

4 slices of bread

freshly ground black pepper

serves 2–4

Melt the butter in a heavy-based saucepan, add the onion and cook until it has softened. Add the Cheddar, ale, mustard and salt. Stir over low heat until the cheese has melted.

Add the eggs and stir until the mixture has thickened slightly, about 2–3 minutes. Don't overcook or you will end up with scrambled eggs.

Toast the bread on both sides, then spoon the cheese mixture onto the toast and cook under a hot grill, until puffed and gold-flecked. Serve with lots of black pepper.

Homemade sausage rolls are relatively quick and easy to make, and they are delicious served warm from the oven. These snack-sized sausage rolls are ideal for gatherings with family and friends over the Christmas period.

sausage rolls

500 g chilled fresh ready-made puff pastry

500 g pork sausagemeat

plain flour, to dust

milk or beaten egg, to glaze

makes about 40

Preheat the oven to 220°C (425°F) Gas 7.

Remove the pastry from the refrigerator about 20 minutes before using. Cut the block of pastry in half. Roll out one piece of pastry on a lightly floured surface to form a rectangle about 42 x 20 cm. Cut the pastry rectangle in half lengthways to form 2 equal-sized strips.

Divide the sausagemeat into 4 equal pieces. On a lightly floured surface, roll out 2 of the sausagemeat portions into long rolls, each the length of the pastry strips.

Lay a sausagemeat roll lengthways on each strip of pastry. Brush the pastry edges with a little water, then fold one side of the pastry over the sausagemeat and press the long edges together to seal using the tines of a fork – this will also add a decorative edge to the sausage rolls.

Repeat with the remaining pastry and sausagemeat. Trim the ends of each long roll. Lightly brush the pastry all over with milk to glaze, then cut each long roll into 4-cm lengths. Using a sharp knife, make a slit in the top of each sausage roll.

Transfer the sausage rolls to two baking sheets, leaving a space between each one. Bake for 15 minutes, then reduce the oven temperature to 180°C (350°F) Gas 4, and bake for a further 10–15 minutes, or until the sausage rolls are deep golden, crisp and cooked. Transfer to a wire rack to cool and serve warm or cold.

What could be more British than creamy, crumbly Stilton, the king of English cheese? The combination of pear and Stilton in this starter works wonderfully, both visually and on the taste buds.

sweet pear and stilton melt

4 firm, ripe pears, halved lengthways and cored

2 tablespoons freshly squeezed orange juice

70 g Stilton cheese, crumbled

1 tablespoon dried cranberries or sultanas

1 tablespoon toasted chopped hazelnuts

2 teaspoons finely grated unwaxed orange zest

1 tablespoon extra virgin olive oil

4 handfuls of bitter salad leaves

sea salt and freshly ground black pepper

serves 4

Preheat the grill to medium and line the grill tray with aluminium foil.

Brush the pear halves with a little orange juice. Put the Stilton in a bowl and beat with a wooden spoon until creamy. Stir in the cranberries, hazelnuts, orange zest and enough orange juice to moisten. Fill the pear hollows with the cheese mixture.

Transfer the pears to the grill tray and grill for 3–4 minutes, or until the cheese just begins to melt. Remove from the heat.

Put the olive oil, remaining orange juice and seasoning to taste, in a large bowl. Beat well. Add the salad leaves and toss to coat. Divide the salad leaves between 4 serving plates. Put 2 pear halves on each plate and serve immediately.

variation Leave the pears whole. Core them with an apple corer and brush with lemon juice to prevent discolouration. Make the filling as above and use to stuff the pears, filling from the base. Chill for at least 30 minutes, then serve on the dressed salad leaves.

Treated properly, parsley, garlic and extra virgin olive oil can create a superb, vividly scented green oil which will make any seafood taste good. Drizzled over scallops, which have been briefly marinated in lemon juice and lovely olive oil, it becomes a sensational recipe.

char-grilled scallops
with parsley oil

2 garlic cloves, peeled and crushed

4 tablespoons extra virgin olive oil

juice of 1 lemon

375–400 g plump fresh scallops, about 16

a small handful of fresh chives (optional), to serve

parsley oil

a small bunch of fresh parsley, finely chopped, about 15 g

125 ml extra virgin olive oil

1 garlic clove, peeled and crushed

sea salt and freshly ground black pepper

8 short wooden skewers or satay sticks, soaked in water for 30 minutes

serves 4

Mix the garlic, olive oil and lemon juice in a shallow, non-metal dish. Pat the scallops dry with kitchen paper. Make shallow criss-cross cuts in each one. Prick the corals with a toothpick to prevent splitting. Add the scallops to the dish of marinade, turning once and set aside while you prepare the parsley oil.

To make the parsley oil, put the parsley, olive oil and garlic in a blender and blend until smooth. Strain into a bowl or just pour straight from the blender and use this vivid green oil as both garnish and condiment.

Drain the scallops, then thread two onto each skewer. Pour the marinade into a frying pan, bring to the boil and cook until reduced to a sticky golden glaze. Add the scallops and sizzle them in the glaze for 1 minute on each side (or a little longer if preferred). Serve drizzled with parsley oil and a separate small dish of oil for dipping. Sprinkle with seasoning and decorate with a bundle of chives, if using.

note Try to buy fresh local scallops on the shell – get your fishmonger to prepare them. If buying scallops out of the shell, do not buy any that are sitting in water. The water soaks into the flesh and when the scallops hit the pan, the water seeps out and makes the scallops mushy.

The salty, smoky taste of salmon blends well with the starchy texture of potatoes. Broad beans are one of the few foods that don't seem to suffer from the freezing process. In fact, since they're frozen almost as soon as they're picked, their texture can often be better than those you buy at the market. Like most green vegetables, broad beans are very good cooked in a microwave.

smoked salmon salad

Microwave the broad beans on HIGH for 3 minutes if fresh, or 2 minutes if frozen. Transfer immediately to a bowl of iced water. When cold, pop them out of their grey skins, discard the skins and reserve the beans.

Boil the potatoes whole, in their skins, until tender, about 15–20 minutes (the time depends on the size of the potatoes). Drain, then toss in 2–3 teaspoons of the olive oil (gently so as not to break the skins). Cut the potatoes in half and arrange on 4 chilled plates. Top with the broad beans and smoked salmon. Sprinkle with seasoning and the chives. Drizzle with about 1 tablespoon olive oil per plate and sprinkle with 1 teaspoon cider vinegar.

250 g shelled broad beans, fresh or frozen

12 baby red potatoes

4–5 tablespoons extra virgin olive oil

100 g smoked salmon, diced

a handful of fresh chives, snipped

4 teaspoons cider vinegar, white wine vinegar or rice vinegar

sea salt and freshly ground black pepper

serves 4

The freshest, crispest green vegetables, like peas, beans, courgettes, asparagus and their kin, bought in season when they are at their peak, make a fantastic, satisfying salad. They marry particularly well with the milder members of the onion family – pearl onions, baby spring onions or red onion.

green vegetable salad
with hazelnut dressing

about 12 mini asparagus tips

a handful of mini green beans (untrimmed)

4 mini courgettes, cut into thirds lengthways (optional)

100 g sugar snap peas

100 g shelled green peas

100 g mini spring onions

hazelnut oil, to drizzle

75 g hazelnuts, pan-toasted in a dry frying pan, then lightly crushed into halves or big pieces

sea salt and freshly ground black pepper

fresh Parmesan cheese, to serve

hazelnut dressing

6 parts extra virgin olive oil

1 part white wine vinegar

½ teaspoon mustard

serves 4

Microwave the asparagus tips, beans, courgettes, sugar snaps and green peas separately, on HIGH, for 2 minutes each, then transfer immediately to a bowl of iced water. Alternatively, bring a large saucepan of water to the boil, then add each vegetable and blanch until just tender, but still al dente. Keep the peas until the end, and drain well before chilling.

To make the hazelnut dressing, put the olive oil, vinegar, mustard, and seasoning in a salad bowl and beat well with a fork or small whisk to form an emulsion. Put in a bowl, add the drained vegetables and toss until lightly coated. Arrange the vegetables on a serving platter or four salad plates, then drizzle with hazelnut oil and top with toasted hazelnuts. Shave fresh Parmesan over the top and finish with seasoning, to taste.

note Nut oils and nuts become rancid very quickly, so buy them in small quantities. Use them quickly, keep them sealed and store in the refrigerator, returning to room temperature for serving.

A splendid summery take on roast beef – perfect as a special-occasion salad for a summer lunch party. For the best flavour, let the meat return to room temperature first. Don't salt it first, or you'll draw out the juices. Serve with beef's ideal accompaniment – finest homemade Horseradish Sauce (page 125).

rare beef salad
with watercress

olive oil, to grease

1 beef fillet, about 50 cm long, well trimmed

500 g watercress or other peppery leaves, such as wild rocket or wild garlic (rampion)

Horseradish Sauce (page 125), to serve

sea salt and freshly ground black pepper

serves 8

Preheat the oven to 200°C (400°F) Gas 6.

Brush a heavy-based roasting tin with olive oil and heat on top of the stove until very hot. Add the beef and seal on all sides until nicely browned. Transfer to the oven and roast for 20 minutes. Remove from the oven and set aside to fix the juices. Season.

Leave the meat to cool to room temperature and reserve any cooking juices. If preparing in advance, wrap closely in aluminium foil and chill, but return it to room temperature before serving.

Arrange the leaves down the middle of a rectangular or oval serving dish. Slice the beef into 1-cm thick slices with a very sharp carving knife (or an electric knife). Arrange in overlapping slices on top of the leaves and pour over any cooking juices from the roasting tin or carving board.

Serve with Horseradish Sauce.

This salad makes a wonderful starter or supper dish. Be careful not to overcook the chicken livers, or they will become dry and tough, instead of perfectly cooked, juicy and soft. Chicken livers are available in butcher's shops and large supermarkets, fresh or frozen.

chicken liver salad

4 slices toasted or fried bread

200 g mixed lettuce leaves

200 g chicken livers

50 g butter

2 tablespoons olive oil

100 ml red wine

sea salt and freshly ground black pepper

serves 4

Put the toast on 4 small salad plates and top with the lettuce leaves.

Trim the chicken livers, removing any tubes and any dark or slightly green patches. Cut the livers into equal pieces.

Melt the butter and olive oil in a large saucepan. When really hot, add the chicken livers and cook for 2 minutes on one side, then turn them over and cook for 2 minutes more.

Season, then carefully remove the livers from the saucepan, using a slotted spoon, and divide them between the plates, laying them on top of the lettuce leaves.

Add the wine to the pan juices and bring to the boil, stirring. Boil hard for 1 minute, then pour the hot dressing over the livers and serve.

fish

500 ml milk

750 g smoked or fresh haddock, skinned

275 g unsalted butter

1 tablespoon English mustard powder

4 tablespoons plain flour

2 hard-boiled eggs, peeled and quartered

1 kg floury potatoes

sea salt and freshly ground black pepper

serves 4

Nothing beats a steaming, creamy fish pie on a cold winter's evening. The hint of mustard and boiled eggs lift this from a safe supper dish to a fantastic winner of a pie.

traditional fish pie

Preheat the oven to 200°C (400°F) Gas 6.

Put the milk in a wide saucepan, heat just to boiling point, then add the fish. Turn off the heat and leave the fish to poach until opaque – do not over-cook.

Meanwhile, melt 125 g of the butter in another saucepan, then stir in the mustard and flour. Remove from the heat and strain the poaching liquid into the pan.

Arrange the fish and eggs in a shallow pie dish or casserole.

Return the pan to the heat and, whisking vigorously to smooth out any lumps, bring the mixture to the boil. Season to taste. (Take care: if you are using smoked fish, it may be salty enough.) Pour the sauce into the casserole and mix carefully with the fish and eggs.

Cook the potatoes in boiling salted water until soft, then drain. Return to the pan. Melt the remaining 150 g butter in a small saucepan. Reserve 4 tablespoons of this butter and stir the remainder into the potatoes. Mash well and season. Spoon the mixture carefully over the sauced fish, brush with the reserved butter and transfer to the oven. Cook for 20 minutes, or until nicely browned.

note If you can't find smoked haddock, you can sprinkle 125 g smoked salmon, finely sliced, over the poached fresh haddock just before adding the sauce.

This classic Anglo-Indian recipe began life in colonial India as a breakfast dish, but nowadays it is great whatever time of day you choose to make it.

kedgeree

450 g undyed smoked haddock fillets

2 bay leaves

120 g basmati rice

3 tablespoons olive oil

5 spring onions, finely chopped

1–2 garlic cloves, peeled and finely chopped

1–1½ tablespoons curry powder

freshly squeezed juice of 1 lemon

2 hard-boiled eggs

2 tablespoons chopped fresh coriander

freshly ground black pepper

lemon wedges, to serve

serves 4

Put the haddock, bay leaves and 100 ml water in a frying pan and bring to the boil. Cover, reduce the heat and simmer for 5 minutes. Remove the pan from the heat, drain and, when cool enough to handle, remove the skin from the fish and flake the flesh with a fork. Set aside.

Meanwhile, bring a large saucepan of water to the boil. Add the rice and return to the boil. Stir, then reduce the heat and simmer for 10 minutes, until the rice is cooked but still has a slight bite to it. Drain and reserve.

Heat a large, non-stick frying pan. Add the oil, spring onions and garlic and fry gently until softened and slightly coloured, about 6 minutes. Add the curry powder and cook for 2 minutes. Add the lemon juice, the reserved haddock and rice. Cut one egg into wedges and reserve. Chop the other one into small pieces and add to the pan. Sprinkle with the coriander and season to taste with pepper. Continue to heat, stirring gently, until piping hot.

Transfer the kedgeree to a warm serving dish. Top with the egg and lemon wedges and serve immediately.

variation Use 400 g fresh salmon fillets instead of the haddock and cook as above. Alternatively, add 75 g smoked salmon, cut into thin strips, at the same time as the chopped egg.

5 tablespoons olive oil

3 garlic cloves, peeled and chopped

2 onions, chopped

2 leeks, trimmed and sliced

3 celery sticks, sliced

1 fennel bulb, trimmed and sliced

1 tablespoon plain flour

1 bay leaf

a sprig of fresh thyme

a generous pinch of saffron threads

three 410-g tins chopped tomatoes

2 litres fish stock

1 kg monkfish tail, cut into 8 pieces

500 g mussels in shells, scrubbed

8 scallops

8 uncooked prawns, shell on

a bunch of fresh flat leaf parsley, chopped

sea salt and freshly ground black pepper

serves 8

Make this on a summer's day for a taste of the seaside. Don't forget to provide a few empty dishes for discarded shells and some bowls of warm water with lemon slices for washing fingers.

easy fish stew

Heat the oil in a large saucepan and add the garlic, onions, leeks, celery and fennel. Cook over low to medium heat for 10 minutes until soft.

Sprinkle in the flour and stir well. Add the bay leaf, thyme, saffron, tomatoes and fish stock, and season to taste. Bring to the boil, then simmer for 25 minutes.

Add the monkfish, mussels, scallops and prawns, cover with a lid and simmer very gently for 6 minutes. Remove from the heat and set aside, with the lid on, for 4 minutes. Add the parsley and serve with plenty of warm crusty bread.

This traditional Scottish stew – known as Cullen Skink – is made with smoked Finnan haddock, thickened with potatoes and enriched with a splash of cream. If you can't get this fish, use another naturally smoked haddock instead – but not the artificially dyed variety!

smoked haddock stew
with potatoes and celeriac

25 g unsalted butter

2 onions, finely chopped

250 g potatoes, diced

1 celeriac, about 500 g, finely chopped

250 ml fish stock

500 ml hot milk

1 kg undyed smoked haddock, preferably Finnan

about 150 ml double cream

a large handful of fresh parsley, chopped, to serve

sea salt and freshly ground black pepper

serves 4

Preheat the oven to 150°C (300°F) Gas 2.

Heat the butter in a large saucepan, add the onions, potatoes and celeriac and cook, stirring until softened. Add the fish stock, 250 ml water and pepper. Bring to the boil, then pour into a casserole.

Cover and cook in the preheated oven for 50 minutes, or until the potatoes and celeriac have disintegrated into the liquid and the mixture has thickened. Remove from the oven.

Pour the milk into the casserole. Put the smoked haddock, skin-side up, on top of the vegetables and return to the oven for a further 4–5 minutes, or until the fish is cooked. Remove from the oven and take out the haddock. Peel off and discard the skin and bones. Flake the fish with a fork and set aside.

Stir the cream into the casserole and reheat. Return the fish to the casserole, then serve in deep dishes with the chopped parsley.

variation For a smoother soup-stew, after removing the fish from the casserole, press the remaining mixture through a coarse sieve. Proceed with the recipe and add extra milk or cream, if necessary.

Celery leaf makes a delicious herb, and plants are now available in pots from garden centres. You could also use the pale leaves growing inside an ordinary head of celery. Celery and flat leaf parsley leaves are perfect crisply fried and curly parsley is also good. Chervil and parsley are used to flavour the coating on the fish.

crisp-fried herbed halibut
with shoestring potatoes

750 g waxy potatoes, such as Belle de Fontenay

sunflower oil, for deep-frying

1 egg white

1 tablespoon milk

750 g halibut fillet, cut into 8 pieces

3 sprigs of fresh chervil

3 sprigs of fresh flat leaf parsley

100 g plain flour

1 teaspoon black sesame seeds

½ teaspoon chilli powder

sea salt and freshly ground white pepper

an electric deep-fryer

serves 4

Using a mandolin, cut the potatoes as thinly as possible into strips, then put into a bowl of cold water to rinse off the starch. Drain and dry well with kitchen paper.

Fill a deep-fryer with sunflower oil to the manufacturer's recommended level and heat to 180°C (350°F). Working in batches, fry the potatoes until golden, then drain on kitchen paper. Keep hot.

Put the egg white and milk in a bowl and mix. Rub the fish with the egg white mixture. Finely chop the leaves from the chervil and parsley.

Sift the flour into a bowl, then add the chopped chervil and parsley, the sesame seeds, chilli powder and seasoning.

Deep-fry the celery and parsley leaves. Be careful, they spit furiously, but will be crisp as soon as the spitting stops. Remove and drain on kitchen paper. Dip the fish into the bowl of flour mixture to coat, and fry 2 pieces at a time for 2–3 minutes until just cooked. Drain on kitchen paper and serve with the fried leaves and crisp shoestring potatoes.

This recipe calls for a large piece of cod, the middle cut, known as the saddle. You may have to ask your fishmonger to cut it specially. Save up this recipe for a special meal – it's terribly easy to throw together but looks and tastes impressive.

roast cod
with mustard mash

75 g breadcrumbs

25 g fresh flat leaf parsley, chopped

50 g hazelnuts, crushed

1 kg saddle of cod

sea salt and freshly ground black pepper

mustard mash

1 kg floury potatoes

2 teaspoons English mustard powder, mixed to a paste with 1 tablespoon water

50 g unsalted butter

hot milk

serves 4

Preheat the oven to 200°C (400°F) Gas 6.

Combine the breadcrumbs, parsley and hazelnuts. Put the fish in a roasting tin and press the crumb mixture over the top. Cook in the preheated oven for 25–35 minutes, or until the fish turns milky-white.

To make the mustard mash, cook the potatoes in a pan of boiling salted water until soft and tender. Drain and mash well, stir in the mustard and butter, then beat in enough milk to produce the consistency you prefer.

Serve the cod with the mustard mash and a sprig of parsley.

4 trout fillets
(each weighing about 150 g)

1 tablespoon olive oil

75 g unsalted butter

freshly squeezed juice of 1 lemon

1 tablespoon small capers,
drained and rinsed

1 tablespoon wholegrain mustard

a bunch of fresh tarragon,
chopped

sea salt and freshly ground
black pepper

pan-fried potatoes

900 g new potatoes, scrubbed
and halved if large

2 tablespoons olive oil

25 g unsalted butter (optional)

2 garlic cloves, peeled
and thinly sliced

braised peas and lettuce

25 g unsalted butter

1 onion, finely chopped

2 tablespoons white wine

3 tablespoons crème fraîche

245 g frozen petits pois

1 cos lettuce, shredded

serves 4

All the elements of this meal combine wonderfully to make a satisfying weekday supper. It may seem like there is a lot to prepare but it is really quite easy and the secret is in the timing.

grilled rainbow trout fillets
with mustard and caper butter

To make the pan-fried potatoes, cook the potatoes in a large pan of boiling salted water for about 10 minutes, or until they are just tender. Drain well. Heat the oil with the butter (if using; it gives the potatoes a better flavour) in a large frying pan and add the hot potatoes. Sauté them over medium heat, turning frequently until they are evenly golden brown, about 10–15 minutes. Toss the garlic in for the last 2 minutes of cooking. Drain on kitchen paper, season with salt and serve whilst hot and crispy.

Lay the fish on a lightly-oiled baking sheet, skin-side down. Drizzle with the olive oil and season.

Melt the butter in a small saucepan over low heat and add the lemon juice, capers and mustard. Mix to combine and set aside.

To make the braised peas and lettuce, melt the butter in a pan and cook the onion for 2–3 minutes, or until softened but not coloured. Add the white wine and leave to bubble until the liquid has evaporated. Add the crème fraîche and seasoning. Add the peas and lettuce, and cook for 2–3 minutes, or until the peas are tender and the cos has wilted.

Place the fish under a medium-hot grill for about 4 minutes. Carefully remove from the baking sheet and arrange on warmed plates. Add the chopped tarragon to the butter sauce (at the last moment so that it keeps its vibrant green colour) and immediately pour over the trout.

fish

Originally a way to cook fresh trout brought straight from river to fire, this method lends itself beautifully to cooking a whole fish so that it retains all its flavour and moisture. It looks fantastic and couldn't be simpler!

salmon baked in newspaper

1 fresh salmon, about 1.5 kg, gutted but not scaled

1 unwaxed lemon, sliced

a bunch of fresh herbs, such as dill, tarragon, chervil and bay leaves

4 sheets of uncoloured newspaper

serves 6

Preheat the oven to 200°C (400°F) Gas 6.

Open the newspaper sheets and arrange one on top of each other. Fill a sink with cold water and soak the newspaper in it. Wet a large sheet of greaseproof paper and open it out flat on a work surface.

Put the salmon on top of the greaseproof paper and tuck the lemon slices and herbs into the cavity. Wrap up in the greaseproof paper. Spread the soaked newspaper on the table and put the wrapped fish at the long edge. Roll up, tucking in the sides. Put the fish on a baking sheet and bake for about 45 minutes.

Remove from the oven and unwrap. Test to see if the fish is cooked through (the eye should be white and the flesh opaque to the bone). If not done, wrap up again, spray with water and cook for a further 10 minutes and check after that.

To serve, unwrap the fish and roll onto a serving platter in all its glory. It will taste sublime.

These fish cakes freeze well, so are useful for get-ahead weekends. Any type of fish can be used.

traditional fish cakes

800 g potatoes, peeled

50 g butter

50 ml milk

400 g salmon, cod or halibut, skinned

3 eggs

a bunch of fresh parsley, chopped

100 g plain flour, plus extra to dust

200 g breadcrumbs

300 ml olive oil

sea salt and freshly ground black pepper

lemon wedges, to serve

hollandaise sauce, to serve

serves 4

Preheat the oven to 180°C (350°F) Gas 4 and lightly oil a shallow ovenproof dish.

Cook the potatoes in boiling salted water for 20 minutes, Drain, return to the pan and shake over low heat to dry off. Mash the potatoes, add the butter and milk and mix well.

Put the fish into the prepared dish, cover with aluminium foil and bake for 10 minutes. Leave to cool, then flake the fish into the potato. Beat one egg and add to the mixture, followed by the parsley and seasoning. Mix well.

Put the flour, breadcrumbs and remaining eggs in 3 separate bowls. Whisk the eggs. Divide the fish mixture into 8 equal pieces and shape into patties. Dust each fish cake with flour, then use one hand to dip them into the egg; use the other hand to coat in the breadcrumbs. Try to get an even coating.

Heat the oil and fry the fish cakes on each side for 5 minutes, or until golden. Serve with lemon wedges and hollandaise sauce.

The fish supper has been one of Britain's greatest exports. Crisp, flaky, freshly battered and fried fish (haddock in Scotland; cod in England) and plump, homemade potato chips are cooked in beef dripping or good oil. They are then wrapped in newspaper and eaten in the street, on the quay or carried home. This extremely simple batter is a favourite with many chippies. Typical accompaniments are brown sauce in Scotland, malt vinegar in England, plus salt, pickled onions or gherkins.

fish supper

1 kg floury potatoes, cut lengthways then crossways into 1.5 cm strips (keep in a bowl of iced water until ready to cook)

beef dripping or vegetable oil, for deep-frying

750 g haddock or cod fillets, skinned

sea salt and freshly ground black pepper

beer batter

125 g plain flour, sifted

1 teaspoon salt

250 ml flat beer or water

to serve (optional)

brown sauce or malt vinegar

pickled onions

gherkins

serves 4

To make the beer batter, put the flour, salt and beer in a medium bowl and whisk until smooth.

Drain the potato strips and pat dry with kitchen paper.

Put the dripping in a large, heavy-based, deep frying pan to reach a depth of 2 cm and heat to 200°C (400°F) – use a frying thermometer to check. Add half the potatoes to the pan and fry, turning several times with a spatula, for 10–12 minutes. Remove, drain on sheets of crumpled kitchen paper, and keep hot in a moderate oven while you prepare the rest. Repeat with the remaining potatoes.

Divide the fish into 4 equal portions and pat dry on kitchen paper. Coat the pieces of fish in batter, turning them until well covered. Using tongs, add one portion at a time into the hot fat or oil. Cook until the batter is crisp and golden and the fish just opaque in the middle, about 3 minutes on each side (break one open with a fork to check). Drain on crumpled kitchen paper and keep hot. Repeat with the remaining pieces of fish.

Season and serve with your choice of accompaniments.

poultry and game

The filling for these comforting pies is made with ready-cooked rotisserie chicken (now available at most large supermarkets). The flesh can be shredded and used warm or cold in salads or diced and added to soups, stir-fries and pasta sauces. Don't discard the bones – these can be kept and used to make stock.

chicken pot pies

1 small rotisserie chicken

3 tablespoons butter

1 leek, sliced

1 carrot, diced

1 celery stick, diced

125 ml dry white wine

3 tablespoons plain flour

500 ml chicken stock

100 g frozen peas

125 ml single cream

1 sheet ready-rolled puff pastry, defrosted if frozen

1 egg yolk, beaten with 1 tablespoon water

sea salt and freshly ground black pepper

4 baking dishes, each about 250 ml capacity

serves 4

Preheat the oven to 180°C (350°F) Gas 4.

Remove the skin from the chicken, slice the meat off the bones and chop finely. Set aside until needed.

Melt the butter in a large saucepan set over high heat and add the leek, carrot and celery. Sauté for 5 minutes, until softened. Add the wine and cook for a further 5 minutes, until it has almost evaporated. Add the chicken and stir well to combine. Sprinkle the flour into the pan. Cook for 1 minute, then gradually pour in the stock, stirring constantly as you do so. Bring to the boil and cook uncovered, stirring often, for 2–3 minutes, until the mixture has thickened. Add the peas and cream to the pan and stir well. Cook for 1 minute, then remove from the heat. Season to taste with salt and pepper and let cool to room temperature.

Spoon the mixture into the baking dishes. Unroll the pastry and lay it on a lightly floured work surface. Use a sharp knife to cut circles from the pastry just slightly larger than the top of the dishes. Put a pastry circle on top of each dish, folding the pastry over the side and pressing down firmly with the tines of a fork. Brush with the egg wash and cook in the preheated oven for about 25–30 minutes, until the pastry has puffed up and is golden.

For many people, the smell of roasting chicken conjures up childhood memories of a cosy Sunday at home. It's always worth cooking a larger bird than you need because the leftovers can be used in a pilaf or to make sandwiches. You can also use the carcass to make stock and freeze it. Three meals for the price of one bird!

roast chicken *with lemon, thyme and potato stuffing*

1 medium free-range chicken

1 unwaxed lemon, thinly sliced

4 bay leaves

4 bacon rashers

sea salt and freshly ground black pepper

stuffing

2 garlic cloves, peeled and crushed

1 onion, finely diced

leaves from 4 sprigs of fresh thyme

1 large potato, coarsely grated

300 g sausagemeat

zest and juice of 1 unwaxed lemon

gravy

25 g plain flour

500 ml chicken stock

serves 4

Preheat the oven to 180°C (350°F) Gas 4. Lightly oil a roasting tin.

Take the chicken and carefully slide the lemon slices and bay leaves between the skin and the breast meat.

To make the stuffing, put the garlic, onion, thyme, potato and sausagemeat in a large bowl. Add the lemon zest and juice, season and mix well. Cut any excess fat from the cavity of the chicken, then stuff the bird.

Weigh your chicken to work out the cooking time: you should allow 20 minutes per 500 g, plus 20 minutes extra. Put the chicken in the prepared roasting tin and lay the bacon rashers over the breast. Put in the hot oven and cook for the time you have calculated. When the chicken is ready, remove it from the roasting tin and keep warm.

Now make the gravy. Add the flour to the tin and stir with a wooden spoon to combine with the fat and juices. Slowly pour in the chicken stock, stirring continuously to prevent lumps forming. Put the roasting tin directly on the heat and bring to the boil. When the mixture has thickened, remove it from the heat and season well. If you like a very smooth gravy, press it through a sieve with the back of a spoon.

Family tradition will dictate the best way to present a festive turkey. This recipe uses a fresh chestnut stuffing for the neck cavity. The appeal of roast turkey is as much in the many accompaniments as it is in the meat itself.

traditional roast turkey

1 turkey, 6–7 kg

125 g salted butter

Chestnut Stuffing (page 106)

500 ml chicken or vegetable stock

sea salt and freshly ground black pepper

to serve

Roast Potatoes (page 111)

Bread Sauce (page 106)

Cranberry Relish (page 107)

lightly boiled Brussels sprouts

grilled chipolatas

roasted bacon rolls

squares of muslin, paper or aluminium foil (enough to cover the breast and drumsticks)

serves 6

Preheat the oven to 220°C (425°F) Gas 7.

Wipe out the neck area and cavity of the turkey with a damp cloth and lightly season the inside. Spoon the Chestnut Stuffing into the neck cavity, allowing plenty of room for it to expand.

Put half the butter in a saucepan and melt gently. Spread the remaining butter all over the skin of the turkey. Soak the muslin in the melted butter and drape over the bird, with a double layer of muslin covering the drumsticks.

Put the bird in a large roasting tin in the middle of the oven. Roast for 40 minutes. Reduce the oven temperature to 170°C (325°F) Gas 3 and baste now and every 30 minutes until cooked (remove and replace the muslin as necessary). Roast at this temperature for just under 4 hours.

Raise the oven temperature to 220°C (425°F) Gas 7, remove the coverings and roast for 30 minutes to crisp the skin. Remove the turkey from the oven, cover with a tent of aluminium foil and leave in a warm place to rest while you cook the accompaniments.

Using oven gloves, tip out any free juices from the cavity, then lift the turkey onto a serving platter. Pour off the gravy juices from the tin, preferably into a gravy separator or jug to lift off the fat, then pour in the stock and heat. Serve with the turkey and all the accompaniments.

Ring the changes with this succulent roast goose, perfect as a Christmas lunch. The prunes and apples turn gorgeously soft and sticky after 4 hours inside the roasting bird. Serve with Roast Beetroot (page 117).

roast goose

1 goose, about 6 kg

250 g stoned prunes

500 g tart apples, peeled, cored and quartered

75 ml red wine

1 tablespoon cornflour, mixed with 1 tablespoon water

150–300 ml chicken stock

3–4 tablespoons cream

sea salt and freshly ground black pepper

an instant-read thermometer

serves 6

Dry the goose inside and out with kitchen paper, then rub with salt and pepper and prick the skin all over with a skewer or sharp-pronged fork.

Scald the prunes with boiling water and stuff the goose with the apples and prunes.

Put the goose breast-side up on a rack in a roasting tin. Put in a cold oven, turn to 170°C (325°F) Gas 3 and roast for 45 minutes. Add a little cold water to the tin and roast for 3½ hours or 40 minutes per kilo. Take care not to let the water dry up – add extra as necessary. The goose is done when an instant-read thermometer reaches 82°C (180°F). Alternatively, the juices should run clear when you prick the leg at the thickest part. Waggle the leg bone a little – it should move in the socket. Transfer the bird to a platter.

Reserve 1 tablespoon of the goose fat, pour the gravy juices into a small bowl and stir in the cornflour mixture. Increase the oven temperature to 250°C (500°F) Gas 9. Return the goose to the roasting tin, pour 2 tablespoons cold water over the breast and return the bird to the oven.

Pour the wine into a clean saucepan, add the reserved goose fat, bring to the boil and reduce until syrupy. Add the gravy juices mixture and the stock and return to the boil, stirring all the time. Season well and stir in the cream.

1 venison saddle, about 2 kg,
boned and rolled

stock

½ onion, chopped

250 ml red wine

marinade

60 g softened butter or
4 tablespoons olive oil

12 juniper berries, crushed

½ teaspoon dried thyme

2 garlic cloves,
peeled and crushed

5 salted anchovies, well rinsed,
then chopped

1 tablespoon port

a strip of pork fat or 3 slices
streaky bacon, made into
long rolls

3 sprigs of fresh rosemary

sea salt and freshly ground
black pepper

gravy

1 tablespoon redcurrant jelly

1 tablespoon cornflour, mixed
with 125 ml water

kitchen string

an instant-read thermometer

serves 8–10

Venison is an umbrella word covering the meat of many kinds of deer. The saddle of these animals is almost always tender but it is still a good idea to tenderize the meat further by hanging it for a while. A good butcher will often do this for you.

marinated roast venison

Open the saddle and cut away all the loose trimmings around the rib area and any excess flank, leaving enough to wrap around the meat. To make a stock, put the trimmings, onion, red wine and 500 ml water in a saucepan. Bring to the boil, reduce the heat and simmer gently for 1 hour.

To make the marinade, put the butter, juniper berries, thyme, garlic, anchovies and seasoning in a bowl and mix well. Put the opened saddle in a roasting tin, rub with half the marinade and sprinkle with the port. Arrange the rolled pork fat lengthways along the backbone cavity, top with the sprigs of rosemary, close the meat up and tie it with string. Rub the outside with the rest of the marinade, wrap the meat in foil or greaseproof paper and leave in a cool place for at least 3 hours.

Preheat the oven to 250°C (450°F) Gas 7.

Unwrap the meat and roast for 10 minutes, then reduce to 170°C (325°F) Gas 3 for 45 minutes, or until an instant-read thermometer registers 65°C (150°F). Baste the meat with the pan juices 2–3 times during this period. Transfer the meat to a serving dish and keep it warm (discard the string).

To make the gravy, put the roasting tin on top of the stove. Add the redcurrant jelly and stock and let it boil until the jelly dissolves, then add the cornflour mixture, return to the boil, season and add any juices collected from the roast. Serve the gravy in a jug. Carve the meat straight across the grain, not lengthways as is often done with a saddle.

Only very young rabbits should be roasted whole, giving the most tender pure white meat imaginable. Otherwise it is best to cut the meat into pieces, frying the legs in butter first to give them a bit of colour, then roasting them with the saddle.

roast rabbit
with herbs and cider

4 wild rabbits, about 500 g each or 2 farmed ones

1 onion, chopped

1 carrot, sliced

1 bay leaf

12 streaky bacon rashers

100 g butter

3 tip sprigs of fresh rosemary, or 1 long one, broken into 3, or 1 teaspoon dried rosemary

6–8 tip sprigs of fresh thyme, 2–3 whole sprigs or ½ teaspoon dried thyme

200 ml cider

2 tablespoons double cream (optional)

sea salt and freshly ground black pepper

an instant-read thermometer

serves 4

First cut the legs and saddle off each rabbit and reserve with the kidneys. To make a stock, put the bones in a saucepan, add the onion, carrot and bay leaf, cover with water and simmer for about 1 hour. Strain off and reserve the stock, discard the bones, and reserve the onion and carrot.

Preheat the oven to 230°C (450°F) Gas 8.

Loosen the tough membrane around the saddles by sliding the point of a sharp knife along the backbone from under the neck end to the tail, freeing the meat underneath. Do one side at a time, then cut off and discard it. Cover the saddle with strips of bacon.

Melt the butter in a frying pan, add the legs and fry for about 5 minutes to give them a bit of colour. Season with salt, pepper, rosemary and thyme. Put the reserved onion and carrot in a roasting tin and set the legs and saddle on top. Roast for 15–20 minutes according to size or until an instant-read thermometer registers 70°C (160°F).

Add the kidneys to the pan used to brown the legs, adding a little extra butter if necessary. Fry gently until firm, then remove and set aside. Deglaze the pan with the cider, add the stock and the cream, if using, and reduce the gravy. Season to taste. Arrange the meat and kidneys on a serving dish and pour the sauce over the top.

Roast guinea fowl is a treat; half chicken, half game, it is full of flavour. Cutting poultry and meat into small pieces means that they roast very quickly and absorb other ingredients more directly, giving great finger-licking potential. This recipe makes for a quick, easy roast to serve for a special meal.

roast guinea fowl
with new potatoes and green beans

1.5 kg guinea fowl

30 g butter

750 g new potatoes

200 g green beans

100 ml vegetable stock

sea salt

radicchio plumes, to serve (optional)

serves 4–6

If using a whole guinea fowl, cut in half lengthways, then cut each half into 6 evenly sized pieces.

Arrange the guinea fowl in a large roasting tin, dot with butter and sprinkle generously with salt. Cover with aluminium foil and leave to stand at room temperature for 1 hour.

Preheat the oven to 200°C (400°F) Gas 6.

Remove the foil and roast for 30 minutes, or until golden brown and tender, turning at least once.

Meanwhile, put the potatoes in a small saucepan of salted water and boil until tender, then drain. Cook the beans in the same way for about 8 minutes until al dente, then drain.

Add the potatoes and beans to the roasting dish and stir well to coat with the pan juices. Transfer the meat and vegetables to a serving plate.

Deglaze the tin with the stock, boil until reduced by half, then pour over the meat and vegetables. Serve with radicchio plumes, if using.

meat

Serve this with beef's stalwart companions – Yorkshire puddings, horseradish sauce and lots of gravy.

roast beef
with all the trimmings

3 kg bone-in forerib of beef (2–3 bones)

2 tablespoons plain flour

1 tablespoon hot mustard powder

75 g beef dripping, shortening or 4 tablespoons olive oil

3 onions, quartered

8–10 potatoes, cut into chunks and par-boiled

5–6 parsnips, halved lengthways

sea salt and freshly ground black pepper

to serve

Yorkshire Puddings (page 125)

Horseradish Sauce (page 125)

1.25 kg green vegetable, such as cabbage, sliced and steamed or boiled

1 recipe Gravy (page 107)

an instant-read thermometer

serves 8–10

Preheat the oven to 240°C (475°F) Gas 8.

Season the meat, mix the flour and the mustard and pat it onto the beef fat. Put the dripping in a roasting tin, put the onions in the middle and set the beef, fat-side up, on top. Put the potatoes and parsnips around the meat and put the tin in the oven. Roast for 35 minutes.

Reduce the oven temperature to 190°C (375°F) Gas 5, baste the beef and turn the potatoes and parsnips in the fat. Keep basting and turning the vegetables every 15 minutes. Roast for 70 minutes.

Increase the oven temperature to 240°C (475°F) Gas 8 and roast for the last 10 minutes' cooking time.

Remove the beef from the oven, or when an instant-read thermometer registers 60°C (175°F) (or a little below if you like beef very rare). Lift the beef onto a serving dish and set aside in a warm place for 20 minutes. It will go on cooking as it rests.

Spoon off the fat from the roasting tin and retain it for another time, or use for the Yorkshire puddings.

Serve the beef with the horseradish sauce, Yorkshire puddings, green vegetables and gravy.

This dish is absolutely delicious, a real winner for either an informal dinner party or just a mid-week supper. What's more, it's an absolute breeze to make. Stilton is the ideal accompaniment to the succulent steak.

stilton steaks *with sweet potato and garlic mash*

600 g sweet potatoes, peeled and cut into chunks

200 g potatoes, peeled and cut into chunks

2–3 garlic cloves, peeled

4 sirloin steaks, about 225 g each

70 g Stilton cheese

1 tablespoon olive oil

6 fresh oregano sprigs, chopped

sea salt and freshly ground black pepper

serves 4

Bring a large saucepan of lightly salted water to the boil. Add the sweet potatoes, potatoes and garlic. Cook until tender, about 20 minutes.

Cook the steaks under a hot grill for 8–10 minutes, depending on personal preference, turning once halfway through the cooking time. Divide the Stilton into 4 equal pieces and crumble over the top of the steaks a couple of minutes before removing them from the grill. Keep them warm in a low oven.

Drain the potatoes, reserving 60 ml of the cooking water. Return the potatoes and garlic to the warm saucepan. Add the oil and most of the oregano and season with salt and pepper. Mash well, adding a little of the reserved cooking water to moisten, if necessary.

Divide the mash between 4 warm serving plates and put the Stilton steaks on top. Sprinkle with some oregano leaves and serve immediately.

variation When in season, replace the potatoes with the equivalent weight of peeled Jerusalem artichokes.

Think of chilly, dark evenings and this is exactly what you'd want to eat. The feather-light dumplings nestling in the rich, savoury casserole will have everyone demanding more. A staple of British cooking.

beef and carrot casserole
with cheesy dumplings

1 tablespoon olive oil

2 garlic cloves, peeled and crushed

1 onion, diced

2 celery sticks, diced

800 g chuck steak, cut into cubes

400 ml beef stock

200 ml red wine

2 bay leaves

4 carrots, cut into small chunks

25 g plain flour

sea salt and freshly ground black pepper

dumplings

200 g plain flour

75 g hard vegetable fat

1 teaspoon baking powder

75 g strong Cheddar cheese, grated

serves 4–6

Heat the olive oil in a large casserole, add the garlic, onion and celery and sauté for 4 minutes. Transfer to a plate. Put the beef in the casserole, increase the heat and sauté for 5 minutes, stirring frequently. When the beef is cooked, return the onion mixture to the casserole. Add the stock, red wine, seasoning and bay leaves, bring to the boil, then reduce the heat to a gentle simmer. Cover and cook for 1½ hours.

To make the dumplings, place the flour and baking powder in a bowl and rub in the fat until it resembles breadcrumbs. Add the cheese, mixing it in with a knife. Add 75–100 ml water and use your hands to bring the mixture together and form a dough. Divide into 8 equal pieces and roll into balls.

Remove the casserole from the heat for 5 minutes, then sift in the flour and stir to thicken the gravy. Return to the heat, add the carrots and stir until the casserole comes to a simmer. Place the dumplings on top, cover and cook for a further 20 minutes.

Here's an Irish twist on a Belgian classic. Carbonnade is usually flavoured with beer but a good Irish stout works particularly well, adding an extra dimension of bitterness to counter the naturally sweet gravy. Lots of shallots also add to the sweetness here. Serve with mounds of creamy mashed potatoes.

irish carbonnade

2 tablespoons duck or goose fat, or peanut or sunflower oil

750 g skirt steak or casserole beef, cut into 3-cm cubes

3 tablespoons sugar

1 onion, chopped

2 tablespoons plain flour

12 shallots

500 ml hot beef stock

375 ml stout, such as Guinness

2 tablespoons red wine vinegar

3 cloves

2 bay leaves

sea salt and freshly ground black pepper

serves 4

Heat the fat in a large frying pan. Season the meat, add to the pan and sauté until browned all over. Transfer to a large flameproof casserole.

Add the sugar to the frying pan and let it cook until it becomes a good chestnut colour. Add the onion, flour and shallots and mix well for about 30 seconds. Stir in the stock and stout. Bring to the boil and cook for 1 minute. Add the vinegar, cloves, bay leaves and a little more seasoning, then pour it all over the meat in the casserole. Mix well.

Cover the casserole and leave to simmer very gently on the stove or in a preheated oven at 170°C (325°F) Gas 3 for 1½–2 hours. Remove from the heat or the oven and pour off the liquid into a separate saucepan or frying pan. Bring to the boil and simmer to reduce the liquid to a coating consistency. Return it to the casserole and serve.

A British classic, with many subtle variations. This one is served with a rich mustard sauce to complete the dish.

beef wellington

4 tablespoons olive oil

3 shallots, finely chopped

2 garlic cloves, peeled and chopped

150 g portobello mushrooms, sliced

1.25 kg fillet of beef, trimmed

500 g puff or shortcrust pastry

2 eggs, beaten

sea salt and freshly ground black pepper

mustard sauce

2 tablespoons mustard

2 tablespoons wholegrain mustard

100 ml white wine

400 ml double cream

serves 8

Put 2 tablespoons of the olive oil into a frying pan, heat gently, then add the shallots, garlic and mushrooms. Cook for 15 minutes, stirring frequently, until soft but not browned and all the liquid has evaporated. Season, leave to cool, then chill.

Preheat the oven to 220°C (425°F) Gas 7.

Put 1 tablespoon of the remaining oil in a roasting tin and heat in the oven for 5 minutes. Rub the beef with the remaining oil and some seasoning, and transfer to the roasting tin. Cook for 15 minutes, then transfer to a plate, reserving the meat juices, and leave to cool.

Roll out the pastry to a rectangle large enough to wrap around the fillet. Brush lightly with the beaten eggs. Spoon the mushroom mixture evenly over the pastry, leaving a 5-cm border all around. Put the cold beef fillet in the middle of the pastry, on top of the mushrooms, and roll the pastry around the fillet. Try not to have too much pastry at the ends, and trim to avoid areas of double pastry. Turn the parcel so that the seam is underneath, and transfer to a lightly oiled baking sheet. Brush all over with the beaten eggs and chill for 2 hours.

Preheat the oven to 200°C (400°F) Gas 6.

Roast for 20 minutes. Reduce the heat to 180°C (350°F) Gas 4 and cook for 15 minutes for rare, 35 minutes for medium and 50 minutes for well done. If you are cooking to well done, you may need to reduce the oven temperature to prevent the pastry from burning.

Put the mustards, wine, double cream and reserved roasting juices into a pan. Bring to the boil, then simmer for 5 minutes. Serve with the beef.

Steak and kidney pudding is British food at its best. Serve wrapped in a linen napkin, with a small jug of extra stock.

steak and kidney pudding

500 g beef kidney, trimmed of any membrane, then cut into 2-cm chunks

4 tablespoons plain flour

1 teaspoon sea salt

1 teaspoon freshly ground black pepper

750 g shin or chuck steak, cut into 3-cm cubes

2 onions, chopped

600 ml beef stock or water

suet crust

500 g self-raising flour

1 teaspoon sea salt

250 g suet or shortening

1 pudding basin, 2.25-litre capacity

kitchen string

serves 4–6

To make the suet crust, put the flour, salt and suet in a bowl and add about 300 ml water, or enough to make a firm mixture. Mix to form a ball. Roll two-thirds of the dough out to a disc 40 cm in diameter. Cut out a wedge from the disc. Line the basin, letting the dough overlap the edges by 2 cm (trim back any excess). Seal any joins with water.

Put the flour, salt and pepper into a plastic bag, seal and shake. Add the steak and kidney to the bag and shake it vigorously until all the meat is evenly coated with the seasoned flour. Remove the meat from the bag, shake off any excess flour and transfer to the basin. Sprinkle with onion.

Heat the stock, season to taste, then pour about half of it over the meat to cover it. Reserve the remaining stock. Roll out the remaining dough to make a disc just big enough to cover the top of the basin.

Fold the overlapping edges of the pastry inwards over the top of the meat and brush the top edge with water. Put the pastry lid on top and crimp the edges inside the rim to seal the pudding.

Fold a large sheet of aluminium foil to make a pleat down the middle. Put on top of the basin and tie a length of string firmly around the edge, under the lip of the basin. Tie a 'handle' of string from side to side to make the pudding easier to lift in and out of the pan.

Lower into a casserole, three-quarters fill the pan with boiling water and cover with a lid. Return to the boil, reduce the heat and simmer for 4 hours (for chuck meat) or 6 hours (for shin meat), topping it up with boiling water from time to time. After the first helping has been served, gently mix in the rest of the stock to thin the gravy for second helpings.

50 g dried wild mushrooms

6 tablespoons olive oil or dripping

1 onion, finely chopped

3 garlic cloves, peeled and chopped

1 large carrot, finely chopped

2 celery sticks, finely chopped

125 g cubed streaky bacon

8 juniper berries, crushed

3 bay leaves

2 tablespoons chopped fresh thyme

2 tablespoons plain flour

1 kg stewing beef, trimmed and cut into large cubes

300 ml red wine

2 tablespoons rowan or redcurrant jelly

600 g ready-rolled puff pastry

1 egg, beaten

sea salt and freshly ground black pepper

6 individual pie dishes or 1 large pie dish

2 baking sheets

serves 6

This glorious recipe can be made as a large pie, or as individual pies for a special occasion. It can be made ahead of time – even frozen. Make the stew in advance, top with pastry and refrigerate until ready to cook.

beef and mushroom pies

Put the mushrooms in a bowl, just cover with hot water and leave to soak for 30 minutes. Meanwhile, heat half the olive oil in a large casserole, add the onion, garlic, carrot and celery and cook for 5–10 minutes until softening. Stir in the bacon and fry with the vegetables until just beginning to brown. Add the juniper berries, bay leaves and thyme, sprinkle in the flour, mix well and set aside.

Heat the remaining olive oil in a large frying pan and fry the beef quickly (in batches) on all sides until crusty and brown. Transfer to the casserole as you go. When done, deglaze the frying pan with the wine, let bubble, then scrape up the sediment from the bottom of the pan. Pour over the meat and vegetables.

Drain the mushrooms and add to the casserole with 150 ml of the soaking water and the rowan jelly. Season, then stir. Bring to the boil on top of the stove, then simmer for 1½ hours. Leave to cool overnight.

Next day, preheat the oven to 220°C (425°F) Gas 7.

Spoon the stew into 6 individual pie dishes. Cut out 6 circles of pastry, a good 3 cm wider than the dishes. Brush the edges of the dishes with beaten egg. Sit the pastry on top of the rim and press over the edge to seal tightly. Brush with more beaten egg, but don't pierce the tops (the steam must be trapped inside). Set the pies on 2 baking sheets and chill for 30 minutes or until ready to bake. Bake for 20–25 minutes, or until the pastry is risen, crisp and golden brown. Serve hot.

250 g pork fillet, diced

125 g pork belly, diced

75 g smoked bacon, diced

25 g chicken livers

1 small onion, minced

1 tablespoon chopped
fresh sage leaves

1 small garlic clove, peeled
and crushed

a pinch of ground mace
or nutmeg

1 red apple, peeled, cored
and diced

sea salt and freshly ground
black pepper

pastry

300 g plain flour,
plus extra to dust

1½ teaspoons salt

60 g white vegetable fat

glaze

1 egg yolk mixed with
1 tablespoon milk

1 jam jar

kitchen string

*6 pieces of waxed paper,
about 30 x 7 cm each*

serves 6

Pork and apple is a delicious combination. These pies are easily transportable and make a wonderful picnic dish.

mini pork and apple pies

Preheat the oven to 190°C (375°F) Gas 5.

Put the pork fillet, pork belly, bacon and chicken livers in a food processor and blend briefly to mince the meat. Transfer to a bowl and mix in the onion, sage, garlic, mace and a little seasoning. Set aside.

To make the pastry, sift the flour and salt in a bowl. Put the fat and 150 ml water in a saucepan and heat gently until the fat melts and the water comes to the boil. Pour the liquid into the flour and, using a wooden spoon, gently draw the flour into the liquid to form a soft dough. Leave to cool for a few minutes and, as soon as the dough is cool enough to handle, knead lightly in the bowl until smooth.

Divide the dough into 8 pieces and roll 6 of these into 12-cm discs. Invert them, one at a time over an upturned jam jar. Wrap a piece of waxed paper around the outside, then tie around the middle with string.

Turn the whole thing over so the pastry is sitting flat. Carefully work the jar up and out of the pastry shell (you may need to slip a small palette knife down between the pastry and the jar to loosen it).

Divide the pork filling into 6 portions and put 1 portion in each pastry shell. Put the diced apple on top. Roll out the remaining 2 pieces of dough and, using a pastry cutter, cut 3 discs from each piece the same size as the top of the pies. Put a pastry disc on top of each pie, press the edges to seal, then turn the edges inwards and over to form a rim.

Brush the tops of the pies with egg-milk glaze. Pierce each one with a fork to let the steam escape. Transfer to a large baking sheet and bake for 45–50 minutes, or until golden. Remove from the oven, transfer to a wire rack, leave to cool and serve cold.

The original humble British comfort food, toad-in-the-hole makes a great Friday night supper dish.

sausage and bacon toad-in-the-hole

175 g flour

2 eggs

150 ml milk

8 streaky bacon rashers

800 g sausages

2 red onions, cut into wedges

sea salt and freshly ground black pepper

serves 4–6

Put the flour in a mixing bowl and make a well in the centre. Whisk the eggs, milk and 150 ml water together and pour into the well. Stir carefully with a wooden spoon until you have a smooth batter. Leave to rest for 30 minutes.

Preheat the oven to 220°C (425°F) Gas 7. Grease a large roasting tin or 4–6 individual dishes and place in the oven.

Wrap the bacon around the sausages and place in the hot roasting tin or dishes. Add the onion, then pour in the batter. Return to the oven and bake for 30 minutes without opening the door. The batter should be light and well risen.

Apple and blackberry is a classic autumn combination best known as a crumble or pie filling but it also works surprisingly well with pork. Be careful not to burn the pan juices, which you then pour over the finished dish.

pork steaks *with apple and blackberry compote*

4 large pork steaks, about 250 g each

50 g butter

12 large fresh sage leaves

sea salt and freshly ground black pepper

apple and blackberry compote

250 g cooking apples, cored and cut into thin wedges

75 g blackberries

2 tablespoons sugar

freshly squeezed juice of ½ lemon

3 juniper berries

serves 4

To make the apple and blackberry compote, put the apples, blackberries, sugar, lemon juice, juniper berries and 2 tablespoons water into a saucepan. Cover and cook gently until the fruits have softened. Remove the lid and simmer until the juices have evaporated. Remove from the heat, but keep the mixture warm.

Season the pork steaks. Melt the butter in a large frying pan and, as soon as it stops foaming, add the pork. Cook over medium heat for 3–4 minutes on each side until browned and cooked through.

Leave to rest in a warm oven for 5 minutes. Meanwhile add the sage to the same pan and fry for a few seconds until crispy. Serve the steaks topped with a spoonful of the compote, the sage leaves and pan juices.

Sometimes this cut is sold without the skin, so it is a good idea to wrap strips of bacon around the meat. The idea is to release some gelatine into the wine to emulsify and combine all the ingredients when you make the gravy. Half a teaspoon of dissolved gelatine added at the end has the same effect, though not the same flavour.

loin of pork *with a herb crust*

Remove the rind if it is still on the pork and put the rind skin-side down in a roasting tin. Alternatively, use unsmoked streaky bacon or omit altogether. Make several small incisions on the underside of the meat and insert the slivers of garlic (use more if you like). Season the meat.

Pour the wine into a plastic bag, add 1 tablespoon of the olive oil, half the thyme, some salt, then finally add the meat. Close the bag, excluding as much air as possible and refrigerate in a dish for at least 2 hours.

Preheat the oven to 250°C (500°F) Gas 9.

Put the meat on top of the rind or bacon in the roasting tin and put in the oven, then reduce the temperature to 180°C (350°F) Gas 4. Baste with the marinade.

Heat the remaining oil in a pan and add the crushed garlic. When it begins to colour, add the breadcrumbs, parsley and remaining thyme.

After 1 hour, remove the meat from the oven and pack the seasoned crumbs on top. Baste carefully with the pan juices. Return to the oven and cook for a further 40 minutes or until an instant-read thermometer registers 80°C (175°F). Lift the meat onto a platter and pour the stock into the pan. Bring to the boil on top of the stove and, if you're not using pork rind, add the gelatine. Season to taste and melt in the jelly. Serve separately in a jug.

1.5 kg loin of pork, chined and trimmed

pork rind or 6–7 slices unsmoked streaky bacon (optional)

2 garlic cloves, 1 cut into slivers, 1 crushed

150 ml red wine

2 tablespoons olive or sunflower oil

2 teaspoons chopped fresh thyme

60 g fresh breadcrumbs

1 tablespoon chopped fresh flat leaf parsley

250 ml beef stock

¼ teaspoon powdered gelatine (optional)

2 teaspoons redcurrant jelly

sea salt and freshly ground black pepper

an instant-read thermometer

serves 4

2 kg blade or hand of pork, with rind if possible, and scored

1 teaspoon sea salt

2 tablespoons olive oil, to glaze

stuffing

1 onion, finely chopped

1 green apple, such as Granny Smith, cut into small pieces

2 celery sticks, finely chopped

60 g cashew nuts, chopped

50 g unsalted butter

2 teaspoons chopped fresh sage leaves

grated zest and freshly squeezed juice of 1 unwaxed lemon

250 g fresh breadcrumbs

cider gravy

125 ml cider vinegar

250 ml water or chicken stock

a roasting tin with a rack

a baking sheet with sides

an instant-read thermometer (optional)

serves 6

This is an ideal cut of pork to serve with crackling. If you can't get the meat with its outer skin on, simply bone and stuff it, and miss out the high roasting part at the end.

rolled crackly pork roast
with sage and onion stuffing

To make the stuffing, put the onion, apple, celery, cashew nuts, butter, sage, lemon zest and juice and breadcrumbs in a bowl. Mix well.

Season the inside of the pork with the salt, then spread the stuffing over that side, roll up the meat and tie it with string to make a good shape. Brush with the oil and put it on a rack in a roasting tin. Add 250 ml water. Put it in a cold oven, turn the heat to 220°C (425°F) Gas 7 and roast for 30 minutes.

Reduce the oven temperature to 170°C (325°F) Gas 3. Cook for another 1½ hours or until an instant-read thermometer registers 80°C (175°F). Transfer the meat to a baking sheet with sides. Do not baste during this time (unless the meat is rindless, in which case, baste 3–4 times during cooking). Raise the oven temperature to maximum and return the meat to the very hot oven for 20 minutes to crisp the surface.

Meanwhile, make the gravy by deglazing the roasting tin with the vinegar and reducing it well. Add the water or stock, bring to the boil, then season with salt if necessary. Serve in a sauceboat. When the meat is ready, transfer it to a carving platter and leave to rest for 10–20 minutes before carving in fairly thick slices.

This lamb is cooked on a bed of rosemary and onions until it is completely tender all the way through – and the onions are melting into the rosemary gravy. Purée the meat juices with the soft onions for a creamy sauce.

pot roast leg of lamb
with rosemary and onion gravy

1.5 kg leg of lamb

2 tablespoons olive oil

3 garlic cloves, peeled and crushed

2 tablespoons chopped fresh rosemary

3 large fresh rosemary sprigs

2 bay leaves

4 large onions, thinly sliced

300 ml dry white wine

2 teaspoons mustard

sea salt and freshly ground black pepper

mint sauce

a large bunch of fresh mint, finely chopped

1 teaspoon caster sugar

2 tablespoons white wine vinegar

serves 6

Trim the lamb of any excess fat. Heat the olive oil in a casserole in which the lamb will fit snugly. Add the lamb and brown it all over. Transfer to a plate and leave to cool.

Preheat the oven to 160°C (325°F) Gas 3. Meanwhile, to make the mint sauce, put the ingredients in a bowl and leave to steep for at least 1 hour.

Crush the garlic and chopped rosemary together with a mortar and pestle. Using a small sharp knife, make little incisions all over the lamb. Push the paste well into these incisions. Season well.

Put the rosemary sprigs, bay leaves and onions in the casserole and put the lamb on top. Mix the wine with the mustard, then pour into the casserole. Bring to the boil, cover tightly, then cook in the oven for 1½ hours, turning the lamb over twice.

Raise the oven temperature to 200°C (400°F) Gas 6 and remove the lid from the casserole. Cook for another 30 minutes.

Carefully remove the lamb to a serving dish and keep it warm. Skim the fat from the cooking juices and remove the bay leaves and rosemary sprigs. Add a little water if too thick, then bring to the boil, scraping the bottom of the pan to mix in the sediment. Pour the sauce into a blender or food processor and blend until smooth. Season to taste. Serve with the freshly made mint sauce.

The preparation and cooking of this dish can be spread over three days, which makes it perfect for Sunday lunch.

lamb shanks *with red wine, rosemary and garlic*

6 even-sized lamb shanks, about 2 kg in total

1 large onion, thinly sliced

3 carrots, cut into thin batons

4 garlic cloves, peeled and thinly sliced

2–3 sprigs of fresh rosemary

½ teaspoon black peppercorns

1 bottle robust red wine, 750 ml, such as Shiraz, Malbec or Zinfandel, plus 125 ml to finish

4 tablespoons olive oil

500 ml passata

sea salt and freshly ground black pepper

Mashed Potatoes (page 112), to serve

a large, heavyweight plastic bag

serves 6

Put the lamb in a large, heavyweight plastic bag. Add the onion, carrots, garlic, rosemary and peppercorns. Pour in the wine, secure the bag, put in a bowl and refrigerate overnight.

The next day, remove the lamb from the marinade, pat dry with kitchen paper and season. Strain the marinade through a sieve into a large bowl and reserve the vegetables. Preheat the oven to 170°C (325°F) Gas 3.

Heat half the olive oil in a large casserole, add the lamb and brown evenly, in batches. Remove the lamb and set it aside. Add the remaining oil to the casserole, then add the reserved vegetables and fry briefly until they begin to soften. Add a few tablespoons of the marinade and let it bubble up, incorporating any caramelized juices that have stuck to the casserole. Stir in the passata and the rest of the marinade, then return the lamb to the pan. Spoon over the vegetables and sauce and bring to simmering point. Cover the meat tightly with greaseproof paper, cover with the lid and cook in the oven for 1¾–2 hours. Remove the lid and paper and cook for a further 30 minutes. Remove the rosemary sprigs, leave to cool, cover and refrigerate overnight.

The next day, remove any fat that has accumulated on the surface. Reheat gently on the stove until the sauce comes to simmering point. If the sauce isn't thick enough, remove the lamb from the pan, simmer the sauce until it thickens, then return the lamb to the pan. Add the remaining 125 ml wine and simmer for a further 15 minutes. Season to taste. Serve with mashed potatoes.

Inspired by thrift, this dish has transcended its humble origins and become a firm favourite around the world. The golden potato topping hides tender lamb in heavenly gravy. A real winter warmer.

lancashire hotpot

2 tablespoons olive oil

800 g lamb neck fillet, cut into 5-cm pieces

1 onion, diced

2 carrots, diced

4 celery sticks, diced

2 leeks, thinly sliced

2 tablespoons plain flour

1 tablespoon Worcestershire sauce

800 g potatoes, unpeeled

sea salt and freshly ground black pepper

serves 4–6

Heat the olive oil in a large, flameproof casserole dish, add the lamb and brown all over. Transfer to a plate. Reduce the heat under the casserole, add all the vegetables, then sauté for 10 minutes, stirring frequently.

Remove the casserole from the heat, add the meat, then sprinkle in the flour and mix well. Pour in just enough hot water to cover the meat and vegetables, stir well and return to the heat.

Preheat the oven to 180°C (350°F) Gas 4.

Bring the casserole to the boil, stirring frequently as the gravy thickens. Season and add the Worcestershire sauce. Remove from the heat.

Slice the potatoes thinly by hand or with a mandolin. Layer them carefully over the meat and vegetables, covering them completely. Place in the oven and cook for 2 hours. The potatoes should be golden on top and the gravy bubbling up around the sides.

30 g unsalted butter or
2 tablespoons sunflower oil

2 onions, chopped

2 garlic cloves

750 g beef mince

70 g bacon, finely chopped

125 ml dry white wine

a handful of fresh flat leaf
parsley, chopped

a fresh thyme sprig,
leaves stripped

2 tablespoons tomato purée

50 g freshly grated
Cheddar cheese

sea salt and freshly ground
black pepper

mashed potato

2 kg potatoes

1 bay leaf

250 ml hot milk

100 g unsalted butter,
cubed

sea salt

a baking dish, about 30 cm long

serves 4–6

The traditional recipe calls for leftover cooked beef, so use that if you have some, but mince that has been well seasoned and cooked in a bit of wine comes a close second. Serve with a fruity red wine.

cottage pie

Preheat the oven to 200°C (400°F) Gas 6.

To make the mashed potato, put the potatoes and bay leaf in a saucepan of cold water. Bring to the boil, add salt and cook until tender. Drain.

Put the potatoes in a large bowl and mash coarsely with a wooden spoon. Using an electric whisk, gradually add the milk and butter, beating until the mixture is smooth. Add salt and whisk well. If the potatoes are very dry, add more milk. Taste, then add more butter and/or salt as necessary and set aside.

Heat the butter in a frying pan, add the onions and cook over high heat until just brown, 3–5 minutes. Add the garlic, beef and bacon and cook until almost completely browned. Add the wine and cook until almost evaporated. Stir in the parsley, thyme leaves and tomato purée. Season to taste.

Spread the beef mixture over the prepared baking dish and level with a spoon. Spread with the potatoes. Sprinkle with the cheese and bake in the oven until golden, about 25–30 minutes.

bread sauce

½ onion, finely chopped

½ teaspoon dried thyme

3 whole cloves

500 ml milk

100 g fresh white breadcrumbs

75 g unsalted butter

2 tablespoons double cream

sea salt and freshly ground
black pepper

serves 8–10

Put the onion, thyme, cloves and
milk in a saucepan. Bring gently to
the boil. Simmer for 5 minutes.
Remove from the heat and leave
for 1 hour. Remove the cloves.
Add the breadcrumbs, butter and
cream. Reheat until nearly boiling.
Stir well, then season to taste. Set
aside for 10 minutes to thicken.

chestnut stuffing

for turkey or goose

400 g fresh chestnuts (200 g peeled
and cooked) or 200 g vacuum-
packed chestnuts, ready peeled
and cooked

250 ml milk (if using fresh chestnuts)

100 g sausages or sausagemeat

2 tablespoons olive oil

1 onion, chopped

150 g turkey liver, chopped
(if unavailable, use chicken livers)

60 g streaky bacon, finely chopped

1 tablespoon chopped fresh flat leaf
parsley or marjoram (optional)

sea salt and freshly ground
black pepper

makes about 500 g stuffing

If the chestnuts are fresh, they
must first be boiled to soften the
shell, then peeled while still hot
(wear rubber gloves to protect
your fingers).

Put the peeled fresh chestnuts in
a saucepan, cover with the milk
and simmer gently until softened,
probably 30 minutes, but it can
take up to 1 hour if they are old.
Strain them if necessary, weigh out
200 g and put in a bowl.

Crumble the cooked chestnuts
with your fingers and use the
sausagemeat to bind them.

Heat the oil in a frying pan, add
the onion, liver and bacon and fry
gently until the liver is firm. Stir in
the parsley and cook until the
mixture begins to brown. Add to
the chestnuts and season to taste.

note This stuffing may also be
cooked separately from the bird.
Form into balls and cook in a
baking dish at 200°C (400°F)
Gas 6 for about 20 minutes.

wine gravy

2 tablespoons fat from the roasting tin used to roast the meat

4 tablespoons red wine

1 tablespoon plain flour (or more if you like a thicker gravy)

500 ml well-flavoured stock or water

sea salt and freshly ground black pepper

serves 4–6

Put the roasting tin on top of the stove, heat the fat, add the wine and reduce to 3 tablespoons. Add the flour, stir well, then pour in the stock. Stir constantly over low heat until the mixture boils. Season. Strain into a clean pan and reheat if necessary.

cranberry relish

100 g fresh cranberries

100 ml cider vinegar

about 3 cm fresh ginger, grated

½ cinnamon stick

2 juniper berries, crushed

2 cloves

50 g demerara sugar

makes about 250 ml relish

Put all the ingredients, except the sugar, in a pan and simmer until the berries collapse (add water if it looks like drying out). Add the sugar and cook for 20 minutes. Remove the cloves and cinnamon stick. It should be like a loose jam. If not, simmer a little longer.

gravy

1 tablespoon fat from the roasting tin used to roast the meat

1 onion, thinly sliced

250 ml good beef stock, or stock to suit the roast meat or poultry

2 teaspoons cornflour, mixed with 2 teaspoons cold water

sea salt and freshly ground black pepper

serves 4–6

Put the roasting tin on top of the stove, heat the fat, add the onion and cook slowly over low heat until browned, about 30 minutes. Add the stock and cornflour mixture, then season to taste. Bring to the boil and simmer for a couple of minutes.

on the side

Every good roast needs the traditional accompaniments to take it to the next level of deliciousness. Roast potatoes are always a favourite at the Sunday lunch table.

roast potatoes

12–16 potatoes, peeled

4 tablespoons duck or goose fat, or olive oil

serves 4

Preheat the oven to 180°C (350°F) Gas 4.

Parboil the potatoes in salted boiling water for 12 minutes, then drain and shake in the colander to roughen up the outsides.

Heat the fat in a large roasting tin in the oven and, when very hot, carefully add the potatoes, turning to coat them in the hot oil. Return to the oven and cook for 40 minutes. Do not disturb them before that or you will spoil their chances of crisping up. Turn them and cook for another 20 minutes.

Mashed potatoes scented with mellowed garlic, cream cheese and good olive oil, are blissful. They marry well with fish but they seem to flatter most meat, poultry and game dishes as well. Use large, floury-textured potatoes for mash – or even waxy if you prefer.

mashed potatoes

1.25 kg boiling potatoes

2 whole heads of garlic, pierced all over with a fork

4 tablespoons cream cheese, about 50 g

4 tablespoons extra virgin olive oil

sea salt and freshly ground black pepper

serves 4–6

If large, cut the peeled potatoes into halves or quarters lengthways. Otherwise, leave whole. Put them in a medium saucepan with the whole heads of garlic and 2 teaspoons sea salt, cover with boiling water, return to the boil and cook for 18–25 minutes, or until tender.

Drain the saucepan well and return the potatoes to the still-hot, dry pan. Slice off the top of the garlic heads, squeeze out the soft purée and add it to the potatoes. Add the cream cheese and extra virgin olive oil. Mash well with a potato masher or large fork or press through a potato ricer. Beat with a wooden spoon until creamy, then season to taste.

Pure comfort food, champ and colcannon are an inextricable part of Irish childhood memories. Dip each forkful of potato in the little pool of butter before eating.

champ

Put the potatoes in boiling salted water and cook for 20–25 minutes, or until tender. Drain well.

Put the spring onions in a saucepan with the milk, bring to the boil, then simmer for 2–3 minutes. Remove from the heat and leave to infuse for 10 minutes.

Mash the potatoes using a potato ricer or mouli, beat in the milk and spring onion mixture, then the butter and some seasoning. Put in a clean pan and reheat. To serve, spoon into small bowls in mounds, make a hollow in the top and insert more butter and blue cheese (if using).

750 g floury potatoes, peeled and cut into large chunks

a bunch of spring onions, including the green tops, chopped

300 ml milk

50 g butter, plus extra to serve

175 g blue cheese, crumbled (optional)

salt and freshly ground black pepper

serves 4

variations **Colcannon, Ireland:** Kale, cabbage or other leafy green vegetable is used instead of the spring onion and cheese. It is served in the same way as champ, or formed into little cakes and fried in butter to form a crunchy crust.

Clapshot, Scotland: Follow the recipe for champ. Omit the cheese and add 750 g mashed swedes. Chives or bacon fat may also be added. The chopped spring onions are optional.

Rumbledethumps, Scottish Borders: 750 g each of cooked potatoes and cabbage are thumped (mashed) then rumbled (mixed) with pepper and 125 g butter, topped with cheese and grilled until brown.

Punchnep, Wales: Half-and-half mashed turnips (neps) and potatoes are heaped into a mound and studded with hollows, which are then filled with cream.

This side dish is as good hot as it is at room temperature. When served hot, it also goes well with roast meat, especially lamb. Cooled, serve as part of a salad selection or a light meal, with a chunk of feta cheese, either crumbled over, or served whole to slice as needed.

roast beetroot

6 beetroot, about 750 g

3 tablespoons balsamic vinegar

2 tablespoons extra virgin olive oil

a small handful of fresh flat leaf parsley, chopped

a small handful of fresh oregano or dill, chopped

a fresh mint sprig, leaves chopped

coarse sea salt

serves 2–4

Preheat the oven to 200°C (400°F) Gas 6.

Peel the beetroot and trim the stems to about 3 cm (don't worry about your fingers, the pink soon goes away). Cut into 4–6 wedges, depending on size. Put the wedges in a baking dish that will hold them in a single layer. Add the vinegar, oil, parsley, oregano, mint and a good pinch of salt. Toss well.

Cover the dish with aluminium foil and roast for 30 minutes. Remove the foil and continue roasting until just tender when pierced with a knife, about 20 minutes more. There should still be some liquid in the dish; if this evaporates too quickly, add a spoonful or so of water during cooking. Serve hot or at room temperature.

Be sure to use a sweet eating apple for this recipe. The cooking variety turns to a purée and spoils the roasting effect. Celeriac must be thickly peeled to remove the tough outer skin. Choose young celeriac, because older ones develop a soft, spongy centre, unlike parsnips, which develop woody cores. Ideally, the centres of both vegetables should be cut away before cooking.

roast apples and celeriac or parsnips

2 tablespoons olive oil

½ teaspoon dried sage

½ teaspoon salt

1 eating apple, cut into wedges

1 celeriac or 2 parsnips, about 350 g, peeled and cut into wedges

1 tablespoon chopped fresh flat leaf parsley

serves 4

Preheat the oven to 220°C (425°F) Gas 7.

Put the oil, sage and salt in a plastic bag, then add the apple and celeriac or parsnips. Roll them around until well coated with oil. Empty the bag onto a baking sheet and roast for 30 minutes, turning the vegetables every 10 minutes. Sprinkle with parsley, mix well and serve.

variation **Parsnip crisps:** Slice 500 g parsnips into thin rounds and coat with olive oil and seasoning. Spread them out on a baking sheet and roast until brown and crisp. Serve with any roast, especially game.

This recipe is a very elegant way to dress up a rustic vegetable. It seems to go best with poultry and potatoes, both roasted. In fact, it's an idea to make extra cabbage and potatoes because they can be mashed together the next day, formed into patties and fried in a mix of butter and olive oil for a leftover feast.

savoy cabbage
with bacon and cream

1 bay leaf

1 Savoy cabbage, about 1.25 kg

2 tablespoons unsalted butter

1 tablespoon extra virgin olive oil

100 g thin bacon rashers, chopped

a fresh sage sprig, leaves stripped and thinly sliced

4 tablespoons double cream

sea salt and freshly ground black pepper

serves 4

Bring a large saucepan of water to the boil with the bay leaf and a large pinch of salt. Quarter the cabbage and blanch in the boiling water for 2–3 minutes. Drain well.

Core the cabbage quarters, then slice crossways.

Heat the butter and oil in a large frying pan. Add the bacon and sage and cook over high heat, stirring often, for 1 minute. Add the cabbage and a pinch of salt and cook, stirring often, for 2–3 minutes.

Stir in the cream and cook until warmed through, about 1 minute. Season well and serve hot.

An ideal – and healthy – accompaniment to most roast meats, this dish is especially versatile because it can be made with baby chard, spinach, mustard greens or rocket. Simply use whatever happens to be in season. Use one of the suggested methods below, whichever suits you best.

wilted greens

750 g greens, mixed or single, such as baby chard, spinach, mustard greens or rocket

extra virgin olive oil

1 lemon

1 garlic clove, peeled (Method two)

fine sea salt and freshly ground black pepper

serves 2–4

Method one (best for larger, robust greens, such as baby chard):
Bring a large saucepan of water to the boil. Salt well, add the greens and blanch for 2–3 minutes. Drain and refresh under cold running water. Leave to dry in a colander, tossing occasionally to let all the water escape (squeeze excess with your hands if necessary). To serve, sprinkle with 2–3 tablespoons olive oil, the juice of ½ lemon and a good sprinkling of salt and pepper.

Method two (best for smaller leaves, such as baby spinach, rocket and mixed baby greens):
Crush the garlic clove, but leave whole and spear on the end of a fork. Heat about 2 tablespoons olive oil in a large pan. Add a very large handful of leaves and cook, stirring with the garlic fork, until wilted. Using tongs, transfer the leaves to a large plate and continue adding handfuls until all the greens are wilted. Season with a trickle of extra oil, a squeeze of lemon juice and a good sprinkling of salt and pepper.

Yorkshire pudding used to be served at the beginning of the meal to fill people up and make the meat 'go further'. These days, it acts as a mop for the gravy and pan juices. If you're lucky enough to have leftovers, they are delicious next day with bacon for breakfast. Fresh horseradish sauce is an eye-opener in more ways than one. Once you've made it yourself, the bottled variety will never be good enough. Grating the horseradish will make your eyes water, but the result is worth it.

yorkshire puddings
and horseradish sauce

275 ml milk

2 whole eggs

125 g plain flour

½ teaspoon salt

4–6 tablespoons fat from the roasting tin

a small roasting tin, 45 x 30 cm, a 6-hole Yorkshire pudding tin, or a 12-hole muffin tin

serves 6

horseradish sauce

1 large horseradish root

1 tablespoon white wine vinegar

250 ml double cream

sea salt

makes about 500–600 ml

Preheat the oven to 230°C (450°F) Gas 8.

Put the milk, eggs, flour and salt in a bowl and whisk well.

Heat the fat on top of the stove in one large tin or divide between a 6-hole tin (1 tablespoon fat for each hole) or a 12-hole tin (½ teaspoon fat for each hole). Pour in the batter (take care because it will spatter). Cook in the oven until well risen (35 minutes for the large tin or 15 minutes for the individual tins). Serve as soon as possible.

To make the horseradish sauce, scrape the fresh horseradish root clean and grate it finely to give 2 tablespoons. Put in a bowl, add the vinegar and salt and stir well. Add the cream and whisk until it becomes thick and light. Rest it at room temperature for at least 2 hours, but serve the same day.

on the side

desserts

Bread and butter pudding is a childhood favourite for many people, and is enjoying something of a revival at the moment. This version is made with tea cakes, in individual dishes, and cooks in under 20 minutes.

bread and butter puddings

300 ml milk

300 ml double cream

½ teaspoon vanilla extract

4 tablespoons caster sugar

3 eggs

6 tea cakes or hot cross buns, halved

50 g sultanas

1 whole nutmeg

6 individual dishes, 200 ml each, well greased

serves 6

Preheat the oven to 180°C (350°F) Gas 4.

Put the milk, cream, vanilla extract and 3 tablespoons of the sugar into a saucepan and heat until the sugar dissolves.

Put the eggs into a bowl, whisk well, stir in 2–3 tablespoons of the hot milk mixture to warm the eggs, then stir in the remainder of the hot milk.

Lightly toast the tea cakes and cut into quarters. Divide between the prepared dishes and sprinkle with the sultanas.

Pour in the custard, grate a little nutmeg over the top, then sprinkle with the remaining sugar. Bake for 18–20 minutes, or until firm. Leave to cool a little, then serve warm.

A British summer classic useful for using up over-ripe berries and slightly stale bread. Now that frozen summer fruits are readily available in most supermarkets, you can enjoy this dessert all year round.

summer pudding

500 g fresh or frozen berries, such as raspberries, blackberries, mulberries or mixed summer berries, thawed, if frozen

2 tablespoons clear honey

125 ml red wine

1 cinnamon stick, bruised

8 slices multi-grain day-old bread, crusts removed

1 teaspoon arrowroot (optional)

a 475-ml bowl or pudding basin

serves 4

If you are using fresh fruit, lightly rinse and leave to dry. Put the berries, honey, red wine, 125 ml water and cinnamon stick in a saucepan and gently simmer over low heat for 5 minutes, until the berries are plump and slightly softened. Remove from the heat and leave to cool. Discard the cinnamon stick.

Cut 6 slices of bread into triangles and use them to line the base and sides of the bowl or basin. Overlap the bread so it completely covers the bowl, leaving no gaps. Reserve the remaining slices. Spoon a little of the berry juice evenly over the bread in the bowl to moisten it. Fill the bowl with the berries, using a slotted spoon. Pack the fruit down with the back of a spoon, taking care not to squash the fruit too much. Cut the remaining slices of bread into triangles. Put these on top of the fruit to make a lid. Reserve any remaining berry juice.

Cover the bowl with clingfilm, put a small plate on top, then put weights on the plate to press it down onto the pudding. Refrigerate overnight.

Remove the weights, plate and clingfilm. Put a plate upside down on top of the bowl. Invert the bowl and plate, then gently remove the bowl.

Put the reserved juice in a saucepan and heat gently. If necessary, gently drizzle the sauce over any parts of the pudding that are not a consistent colour. Blend the arrowroot, if using, with 1 tablespoon of water and stir into the hot juice. Keep stirring until the juice thickens and clears. Pour the sauce over the pudding.

This is a very simple, classic recipe and there are hundreds of versions. Some cook on top of the stove, some call for long grain rice, some add eggs or egg yolks and some add flavourings such as orange peel or cinnamon. The list of things to serve with it is unlimited. Cooked and puréed apples or apricots, chocolate sauce and custard are some traditional favourites.

rice pudding

125 g risotto rice, such as arborio

500 ml whole milk, boiled

60 g sugar

1 vanilla pod, split lengthways with a small sharp knife

15 g unsalted butter

a pinch of salt

serves 4

Preheat the oven to 180°C (350°F) Gas 4.

Put the rice in a saucepan with a lid and add cold water to cover. Slowly bring to the boil over medium heat, then boil for 5 minutes. Drain the rice and rinse under cold water. Set aside to drain well.

Meanwhile, put the milk in an ovenproof pan with a lid and bring to the boil. Add the sugar and vanilla pod. Remove from the heat, cover and leave to stand for 15 minutes. Using the tip of the knife, scrape out the vanilla seeds and stir them through the milk.

Add the rice to the milk, then add the butter and salt. Bring slowly to the boil. Cover and transfer to the oven. Do not stir. Cook until the rice is tender and the liquid is almost completely absorbed but not dry, about 25–35 minutes. Serve warm.

Simple to make yet stunningly beautiful. Choose well-shaped, ripe but very firm pears, so they hold their form during cooking. They work well hot or cold, served with whipped cream studded with ginger and lemon zest.

pears in port
with juniper and ginger

8 Conference pears, peeled and cored but left whole

375 ml red wine, such as merlot

750 ml Ruby Port

1 tablespoon juniper berries, about 20 berries, crushed

zest of 1 unwaxed lemon, cut in a long strip

3 tablespoons caster sugar

3 pieces preserved stem ginger, finely diced, plus 2 tablespoons of the syrup

3 teaspoons arrowroot, blended with 2 tablespoons port

to serve

250 ml double cream, whipped to soft peaks

1 tablespoon syrup from the jar of preserved ginger

finely grated zest of ½ unwaxed lemon

serves 8

Preheat the oven to 150°C (300°F) Gas 2.

Stand the pears upright in a deep, ovenproof dish. Put the wine, port, juniper berries, lemon zest and sugar in a saucepan and bring to the boil, stirring until the sugar dissolves. Pour the mixture over the pears to cover. Stir in the stem ginger and syrup.

Cover and bake for 45–60 minutes, or until the pears are very tender (depending on ripeness). Baste them 2–3 times during cooking.

Remove from the oven and, using a slotted spoon, transfer the pears to a deep bowl.

Pour the cooking liquid into a saucepan and stir in the blended arrowroot until mixed. Bring to the boil, stirring until the wine syrup is smooth and slightly thickened. Remove and discard the lemon zest, then pour the wine syrup over the pears. Serve immediately or refrigerate overnight: the pears will turn a deep purple-red and the spiced wine flavour will intensify dramatically.

To serve, mix the whipped cream, ginger syrup and lemon zest until blended. Serve alongside the pears and drizzle over the wine syrup.

A simple dessert, but somehow deeply satisfying – maybe it's the butterscotch that makes it so irresistible. Since this is always a winner for people with a sweet tooth, make 2 extra apples, for seconds. The combination of dried fruit and cinnamon is reminiscent of Christmas.

baked stuffed apples
with butterscotch sauce

50 g butter

3 tablespoons brown sugar

50 g raisins

100 g dried cranberries

100 g dried cherries

6 cooking apples, such as Bramleys, cored

1 cinnamon stick, broken lengthways into 6 thin strips

Butterscotch Sauce (page 164), warmed

an ovenproof dish, big enough to fit the apples, lightly greased

serves 4

Preheat the oven to 190°C (375°F) Gas 5.

Put the butter and sugar into a bowl, beat until creamy, then stir in the dried fruits. Using a small, sharp knife, score the skin all the way around the middle of each apple, to prevent them bursting. Put the apples into the prepared dish, stuff with the dried fruit mixture and put a piece of cinnamon into each. Bake on the middle shelf of the oven for 20 minutes, then reduce the temperature to 150°C (300°F) Gas 2 and bake for a further 25 minutes, until soft and bubbling.

Serve the baked apples drizzled with the warmed Butterscotch Sauce.

Cranachan is a traditional Scottish dessert marrying oats, whisky, blackberries and cream. It is an easy pudding to put together and chill ahead of time if necessary. This recipe also works well with raspberries or with a mixture of blueberries, blackberries and strawberries. You can always use frozen mixed berries instead. You can also substitute any fruity alcoholic liqueur, such as peach schnapps, Grand Marnier or Cointreau for the whisky.

blackberry cranachan

50 g jumbo porridge oats

25 g soft brown sugar

150 g clotted cream or extra thick cream

2 tablespoons whisky, plus extra to drizzle (optional)

250 g blackberries

2 glasses, to serve

serves 2

Mix the oats and sugar together and spread them out on a baking sheet. Place the sheet under a medium-hot grill. Cook until the sugar has caramelized, stirring the mixture from time to time. Remove from the grill and set aside to cool.

Pour the cream into a large bowl, add the whisky and stir until smooth. Loosely break up the cooled oat mixture between your fingers and add most of the crunchy oats to the cream, reserving a few tablespoons for the top.

Place some of the berries in the bottom of 2 glasses. Spoon a dollop of the cream over the top and then repeat the layers of fruit and cream a second time, finishing with the remaining blackberries.

To finish, sprinkle over the reserved oat mixture and drizzle with a little more whisky, if required.

Crumbles are quintessential British comfort food, best consumed on a miserable winter's night when you need warming up and comforting. If you are using frozen blackberries, there is no need to defrost them first. Bake the crumble in a moderate oven for a long time as this is what gives the topping its wonderful crunch.

classic blackberry and apple crumble

4–5 medium cooking apples (such as Bramley)

250 g fresh or frozen blackberries

4 tablespoons caster sugar

¼ teaspoon mixed spice

finely grated zest and juice of ½ unwaxed lemon

pouring cream or Real English Custard (page 164)

crumble topping

200 g unsalted butter, chilled

200 g plain flour

a pinch of salt

75 g demerara or granulated sugar

a large, shallow, ovenproof dish

serves 6

Preheat the oven to 180°C (350°F) Gas 4 and set a baking sheet on the middle shelf to heat.

Peel, core and slice the apples and put them in a mixing bowl. Add the blackberries, sugar, mixed spice, lemon zest and juice and toss well to mix. Turn into the baking dish.

To make the crumble, rub the butter into the flour with the salt until it resembles rough breadcrumbs. Alternatively do this in a food processor. Stir in the sugar. (At this stage the mixture can be popped into a plastic bag and chilled in the fridge until ready to cook.) Lightly scatter the topping mixture over the apples and blackberries. Place on the baking sheet in the oven and bake for 50–60 minutes.

Remove from the oven and serve warm with pouring cream or Real English Custard.

Summer has truly arrived when gooseberries become available. They seem to have a natural affinity with ginger. Try to track down some ginger wine as it is a delicious tipple and it really brings out the flavour of the gooseberries.

gooseberry and ginger wine crumble

875 g green gooseberries, topped and tailed

3 tablespoons ginger wine

125 g caster sugar

clotted cream, to serve

ginger topping

200 g plain flour

1 teaspoon ground ginger

a pinch of salt

100 g unsalted butter, chilled and cubed

100 g caster sugar

a medium, shallow, ovenproof dish

serves 4

Preheat the oven to 190°C (375°F) Gas 5 and set a baking sheet on the middle shelf to heat.

Put the gooseberries in a non-reactive saucepan, add the ginger wine and sugar and cook gently until the fruit starts to burst. Remove from the heat and tip the gooseberries into a sieve set over a clean pan to catch the juices. Next tip the gooseberries into the baking dish, covering the base with a single layer. Reserve the juices for later.

To make the ginger topping, put the flour, ginger, salt and butter into a food processor and process until it looks like coarse breadcrumbs. (Alternatively you can rub in by hand.) Tip into a mixing bowl and stir in the sugar.

Lightly sprinkle the topping mixture evenly over the prepared gooseberry mixture, mounding it up a little towards the centre. Place the baking dish on top of the baking sheet in the oven and bake for about 25 minutes, until crisp and golden.

Remove from the oven and leave to cool for 5 minutes before serving with the warmed reserved juices and clotted cream.

Here's a traditional British childhood pudding, redolent of school dinners when it was invariably served with lumpy custard. This is a more sophisticated version, with orange to temper the sharp flavour of rhubarb.

rhubarb and orange crumble

Preheat the oven to 200°C (400°F) Gas 6 and set a baking sheet on the middle shelf to heat.

Trim the rhubarb, cut it into large chunks and put in a large saucepan. Finely grate the zest from the oranges and add to the rhubarb. Stir in the ground ginger and sugar and cook over a gentle heat for a few minutes, stirring occasionally until the rhubarb begins to release its juices but is still holding its shape. Pour the rhubarb into a sieve set over a bowl to catch the juices and reserve these for later. Remove the pith from the oranges with a sharp knife then cut out the segments between the membrane. Add to the drained rhubarb, set aside to cool completely.

To make the almond topping, put the flour, salt, ground almonds and butter in a food processor and process until it looks like coarse breadcrumbs. (Alternatively you can rub in by hand.) Tip the mixture into a bowl and stir in the chopped nuts and sugar. (At this stage you can pop it into a plastic bag and chill in the fridge until needed.)

Spoon the rhubarb and oranges into an ovenproof dish or 4 individual ones. Lightly sprinkle the almond mixture evenly over the surface, mounding it up a little towards the centre. Place the baking dish on top of the baking sheet in the oven and bake for about 35 minutes, until crisp and golden.

Remove from the oven and leave to cool for 5 minutes before serving with clotted cream and the warmed reserved juices.

700 g fresh forced rhubarb (for its zing and colour)

2 large unwaxed oranges

a pinch of ground ginger

175 g golden caster sugar

clotted cream, to serve

almond topping

125 g plain flour

pinch of salt

55 g ground almonds

125 g unsalted butter, chilled

125 g blanched almonds, chopped

55 g demerara sugar

a medium, shallow, ovenproof dish or 4 individual dishes

serves 4

Even if you never make puddings at any other time, you probably do when you have people to dinner. Perfect for such an occasion, these little plum fudge puddings can be prepared in advance, then cooked just before serving.

plum fudge puddings

50 g unsalted butter

50 g honey

2 tablespoons double cream

2 tablespoons soft brown sugar

1 teaspoon ground mixed spice

75 g fresh white breadcrumbs

2 ripe plums, halved, stoned and thinly sliced

crème fraîche, to serve

four 150-ml ramekins

serves 4

Preheat the oven to 200°C (400°F) Gas 6.

Put the butter, honey and cream in a saucepan and heat until melted. Put the sugar, spice and breadcrumbs into a bowl and stir well.

Divide half the buttery fudge mixture between the ramekins and top with a layer of plum slices and half the breadcrumb mix. Add the remaining plums and breadcrumbs, then spoon over the remaining sauce.

Set on a baking sheet and bake for 20 minutes. Remove from the oven and leave to cool for 5 minutes, then carefully unmould the puddings and serve with a spoonful of crème fraîche.

An individual white chocolate sponge pudding, baked with a hidden centre of molten chocolate and served with cream, is perfect for any special occasion. It is very important to use the best-quality white and dark chocolate you can find.

white and black puddings

single cream, to serve

dark chocolate filling

75 g dark chocolate, chopped

80 ml double cream

white chocolate sponge

100 g white chocolate, chopped

175 g unsalted butter, at room temperature

150 g golden caster sugar

3 large eggs, beaten

250 g self-raising flour

a pinch of salt

½ teaspoon vanilla extract

about 4 tablespoons milk

an ice cube tray, oiled

6 small pudding moulds, 7.5 cm diameter, well greased

serves 6

The chocolate filling should be made at least 1 hour before making the sponge (though the filling can be kept in the freezer for up to 1 week). Put the chocolate in a heatproof bowl set over a pan of simmering water and melt gently (do not let the base of the bowl touch the water). Remove the bowl from the heat and stir until just smooth. Stir in the cream, then pour into the ice cube tray to make 6 'cubes'. Freeze for at least 1 hour.

Preheat the oven to 180°C (350°F) Gas 4.

When you are ready to make the pudding, melt the white chocolate as above. When melted and smooth, leave to cool.

Put the butter in a bowl and beat the butter until creamy, then gradually beat in the sugar. When the mixture is very light and fluffy, beat in the eggs 1 tablespoon at a time, beating well after each addition. Using a large metal spoon, carefully fold in the flour and salt, then the melted chocolate, vanilla extract and just enough milk to give the mixture a firm dropping consistency. Spoon into the prepared moulds to fill by about half. Turn out the dark chocolate cubes, put one into the centre of each mould, then fill with more sponge mixture to three-quarters full.

Stand the moulds in a roasting tin, cover loosely with well-buttered aluminium foil and bake for 25 minutes, or until just firm to the touch. Run a round-bladed knife inside each mould to loosen the puddings, then carefully turn out onto individual plates. Serve with cream.

A really popular sticky pudding from the Lake District of northern England that is just perfect for a cold day. The toffee sauce is also good with ice cream.

sticky toffee pudding

pudding

175 g stoned dates, chopped

300 ml boiling water

1 teaspoon bicarbonate of soda

50 g unsalted butter, softened

175 g caster sugar

½ teaspoon vanilla extract

2 large free-range eggs, at room temperature, beaten

225 g plain flour

1 teaspoon baking powder

toffee sauce

100 g dark brown muscovado sugar

50 g unsalted butter

200 ml single cream

an ovenproof baking dish, about 1.5 litre capacity, greased

makes 1 large pudding

Preheat the oven to 180°C (350°F) Gas 4.

To make the pudding, put the dates and the boiling water in a small saucepan or heatproof bowl, then stir in the bicarbonate of soda and leave to soak until needed.

Put the butter in a mixing bowl or the bowl of an electric mixer. Add the sugar and vanilla extract and beat until very well combined (the mixture won't look soft and fluffy like a sponge cake mix).

Pour a little of the eggs into the mixing bowl and beat well. Keep on adding the eggs, a little at a time, then beating well, until all the eggs have been used up.

Sift the flour and baking powder into the bowl. Stir gently a few times to half-mix in the flour, then pour the date and water mixture into the bowl. Carefully mix the whole lot together to make a runny batter.

Pour the batter into the prepared baking dish and bake for about 40–45 minutes, or until golden brown. A skewer inserted into the centre should come out clean. If not, give the pudding another 5 minutes in the oven before testing again.

While the pudding is baking, make the toffee sauce. Put the sugar, butter and cream in a small saucepan. Set the pan over low heat and heat gently, stirring now and then until melted, smooth and hot.

Remove the pudding from the oven and serve warm with the hot toffee sauce. Any leftover pudding and sauce can be gently reheated and served again. Eat within 2 days.

A simple cheesecake but all the better for it. You can make curd at home by adding a tablespoon of lemon juice to 600 ml freshly boiled milk, waiting until it separates, then draining off the whey.

yorkshire cheesecake

200 g ready-made shortcrust pastry

250 g curd or cottage cheese

2 tablespoons caster sugar

2 eggs

finely grated zest of 1½ unwaxed lemons

freshly squeezed juice of ½ lemon

2 teaspoons cornflour

2 tablespoons double cream

1 tablespoon butter, melted

40 g raisins or currants, soaked in boiling water for 20 minutes

a deep pie plate, 25 cm diameter or a loose-based tart tin, 23 cm diameter

baking beans (optional)

serves 6

Preheat the oven to 200°C (400°F) Gas 6.

Roll out the pastry thinly on a lightly floured work surface and use to line the pie plate or tart tin, then chill or freeze for 20 minutes. If using a pie plate, make a decorative edge. Cut out a piece of baking parchment to fit the plate or tin and use to line the pastry case, then fill with ceramic baking beans (or rice if you don't have baking beans). Bake for 10 minutes. Remove the baking parchment and beans and return to the oven for a further 5 minutes. Reduce the oven temperature to 180°C (350°F) Gas 4.

Strain the curd cheese in a large bowl. Add the sugar, eggs, lemon zest and lemon juice and, using a wooden spoon or electric hand mixer, beat until smooth. Put the cornflour and cream in another bowl, mix to a smooth paste, then beat into the cheese mixture with the melted butter. Pour the mixture into the pastry case.

Drain the raisins, pat dry with kitchen paper, then sprinkle them over the top of the cheesecake. Bake for 30 minutes, or until set. Leave to cool and serve at cool room temperature.

5 cooking apples, such as Bramley

freshly squeezed juice of 1 lemon

185 g caster sugar,
plus extra to serve

2 teaspoons ground cinnamon

4 whole cloves

milk, to glaze

vanilla ice cream or single cream,
to serve

pastry

325 g plain flour, sifted,
plus extra to dust

a pinch of salt

160 g butter, chilled and cubed

a metal pie plate, 23 cm diameter

serves 4–6

This is such a classic that it barely needs an introduction. Everyone loves apple pie, and cloves and cinnamon elevate this one to another level.

classic apple pie

To make the pastry, put the flour and salt into a large bowl. Working lightly, rub in the butter with your fingertips until the mixture resembles breadcrumbs. Alternatively, use a food processor. Add just enough cold water (about 3–4 tablespoons) to bring the pastry together. Gently form into a ball, wrap in clingfilm and refrigerate for 20 minutes.

Preheat the oven to 220°C (425°F) Gas 7.

Remove the pastry from the refrigerator and divide into 2 balls, one slightly larger than the other. Put the larger piece of dough onto a lightly floured surface and, using a rolling pin, gently flatten it out into a round. Roll out and use to line the pie plate, leaving about 2 cm overhang. Prick the base all over with a fork.

Peel, core and slice the apples into a bowl, tossing them in lemon juice to stop them discolouring. Mix the sugar and cinnamon in a bowl, then put half the apples into the pie plate and sprinkle half the sugar and cinnamon mixture over the top. Arrange the remaining apples on top and sprinkle with the remaining sugar and cinnamon. Dot the cloves on top.

Roll out the remaining pastry and use to cover the pie. Crimp the edges to seal and trim off any excess. Pierce the lid and glaze with a little milk.

Bake for 15 minutes, then reduce the temperature to 180°C (350°F) Gas 4 and bake for a further 25–30 minutes, or until the pastry is golden brown and the apples are well cooked. Sprinkle with extra caster sugar and serve hot with vanilla ice cream or single cream.

A lovely dessert that's quick to make – but remember that it needs 3 hours in the fridge to set. It's pretty, tasty, and healthy too, so no need to feel guilty!

cranberry and raspberry jellies

10 g sheet gelatine
(3 large or 6 small sheets)
or 3 teaspoons powdered gelatine

500 ml cranberry juice

25 g caster sugar

8 cloves

1 cinnamon stick

6 slices fresh ginger

125 g fresh or frozen raspberries

serves 4

Put the gelatine sheets in a bowl of cold water to soften for 5 minutes. Put the cranberry juice, sugar and spices in a saucepan and bring to the boil. Simmer gently for 2–3 minutes, then remove from the heat. Squeeze the excess water from the gelatine, then add to the hot spiced cranberry juice, where it will melt almost instantly. Leave to cool.

Divide the raspberries between 4 glasses and strain the cooled jelly on top. Cover with clingfilm and refrigerate for about 3 hours, or until set.

If using powdered gelatine, measure 4 tablespoons of the cranberry juice in a small bowl and sprinkle the gelatine over the liquid. Leave to swell for 5 minutes while you simmer the remaining cranberry juice, then stir into the hot liquid until dissolved. Leave to cool and continue as above.

Syllabub – a velvety-smooth concoction of sweet wine and cream – is one of the great English puddings, dating from the sixteenth century. This one is made with orange rather than traditional lemon and topped with an irresistibly crunchy mixture of orange zest and sugar.

orange syllabub
with crunchy orange sprinkle

150 ml southern French Muscat or other strong sweet white wine (15 per cent ABV)

1 tablespoon Cointreau or other orange liqueur

finely grated zest of 2 unwaxed oranges

2 tablespoons freshly squeezed orange juice

2 tablespoons freshly squeezed lemon juice

4 tablespoons caster sugar

400 ml double cream, chilled

1 large bowl, chilled for 30–40 minutes in the refrigerator

6 glass dishes

serves 6

Pour the wine into a bowl, add the Cointreau, half the grated orange zest, the orange and lemon juice and 2 tablespoons caster sugar. Stir, cover and refrigerate for several hours or overnight.

Mix the remaining orange zest and sugar in a bowl. Spread it over a plate and leave for a couple of hours to crisp up. Store it in an airtight container until ready to use.

Strain the wine mixture through a fine, non-metallic sieve. Pour the cream into the large chilled bowl and beat with an electric whisk until it starts to thicken. Gradually add the orange-flavoured wine, beating well after each addition until the cream thickens again – you want a thick pouring consistency. When the final addition of wine has been incorporated the mixture should hold a trail when you lift out the beaters, but it shouldn't be stiff. (Don't overbeat it, or it will separate.) Ladle the mixture into the 6 glass dishes and refrigerate for at least 1 hour before serving.

Serve sprinkled with the orange sugar.

Sponge cakes soaked in sherry and topped with fruit, homemade egg custard and cream, create this delicious trifle, which is ideal for an alternative Christmas dessert. Try tinned apricots instead of peaches or 350–400 g thinly sliced Madeira cake instead of the trifle sponge cakes.

old english trifle

8 trifle sponge cakes

115 g raspberry jam

100 g ratafia biscuits or amaretti, lightly crushed

415 g tinned peach slices in fruit juice

100 ml sherry

1 tablespoon cornflour

600 ml whole milk

4 egg yolks

55 g caster sugar

1 teaspoon vanilla extract

300 ml double cream

40 g toasted flaked almonds

a deep glass serving bowl

serves 8

Spread the top of the sponge cakes with jam, then cut them into fingers. Arrange over the base of the serving bowl, covering the base completely. Sprinkle the crushed ratafia biscuits evenly over the top.

Drain the peaches, reserving the juice. Mix together the peach juice and sherry, then pour evenly over the sponge cakes and ratafia biscuits. Arrange the peaches in an even layer over the top. Cover and refrigerate.

Meanwhile, put the cornflour in a heatproof bowl, add 3 tablespoons of the milk and blend together with a whisk until smooth. Add the egg yolks, sugar and vanilla extract and whisk together to mix. Set aside.

Pour the remaining milk in a saucepan and heat gently until almost boiling. Pour the hot milk onto the egg yolk mixture, whisking constantly. Return the mixture to the pan, then cook gently, stirring continuously, until the mixture thickens enough to coat the back of a wooden spoon. Do not allow the mixture to boil as it may curdle.

Remove the pan from the heat and pour the custard into a heatproof bowl. Cover the surface of the hot custard with a piece of greaseproof paper (to prevent a skin forming) and leave to cool completely.

Spoon the cold custard over the peach layer. Lightly whip the cream until it forms soft peaks, then spread cream over the custard, covering it completely. Cover and refrigerate for 3–4 hours before serving. Sprinkle the cream with the flaked almonds, then serve.

225 g fresh white breadcrumbs

55 g plain flour

225 g shredded suet

225 g soft light brown sugar

1½ teaspoons ground mixed spice

225 g sultanas

225 g currants

55 g mixed peel or raisins

55 g flaked or chopped almonds

finely grated zest of
1 unwaxed lemon

1 cooking apple, 200–300 g,
peeled, cored and grated

4 eggs, beaten

3 tablespoons brandy, rum
or sherry

freshly squeezed lemon juice
or milk (optional)

brandy butter

115 g unsalted butter, softened

115 g soft light brown sugar

5–6 tablespoons brandy

*a 1.5–1.6-litre heatproof pudding
basin, greased and base-lined with
non-stick baking parchment*

kitchen string

serves 8

A British Christmas wouldn't be the same without a homemade Christmas pudding. Lovingly prepared up to 8 weeks in advance, it's a boozy pudding best served with lashings of heart-stopping brandy butter.

traditional christmas pudding

Put the breadcrumbs, flour, suet, sugar, mixed spice, sultanas, currants, mixed peel, almonds, lemon zest and apple in a large bowl and stir until well mixed. Add the eggs and brandy and mix thoroughly, adding a little lemon juice to moisten the mixture, if necessary.

Fill the prepared basin with the mixture, pressing down well. Cover the pudding with a disc of greaseproof paper, then cover the basin with greaseproof paper and aluminium foil, pleat them in the centre, then secure under the rim with string.

Put the basin in the top of a steamer. Steam the pudding over a pan of gently simmering water for 5–6 hours, topping up with boiling water periodically so that the pan doesn't boil dry. Remove the pudding from the steamer and leave to cool. Once cold, re-cover with greaseproof paper and foil, and store in a cool, dry, dark place for 6–8 weeks.

On Christmas Day, steam the pudding, as before, for 3–4 hours.

To make the Brandy Butter, put the butter in a bowl and beat with a wooden spoon until it is very soft and creamy. Gradually beat in the sugar until the mixture is very light and fluffy, then beat in the brandy, 1 tablespoon at a time, until well combined. Transfer the mixture to a serving bowl, cover and refrigerate for at least 2–3 hours before serving.

Invert the pudding onto a warmed plate and serve with brandy butter.

This makes a deliciously sticky pouring sauce. For a variation, simply stir in 50 g finely chopped stem ginger.

butterscotch sauce

50 g unsalted butter

75 g soft light brown sugar

50 g granulated sugar

150 g golden syrup

300 ml double cream

½ teaspoon vanilla extract

serves 4–6

Put the butter, soft light brown sugar, granulated sugar and golden syrup in a pan. Stir over low heat until the sugars have dissolved and then bubble gently for 5 minutes, until smooth and thick.

Remove the pan from the heat and stir in the double cream and vanilla extract. Keep warm if using immediately.

There will be more than enough sauce for four servings but it will keep in the fridge for up to a week. Just reheat gently to serve.

This classic creamy sauce is a staple of English cooking – pour generously over crumbles, pies and fruit.

real english custard

1 vanilla pod, split lengthways

300 ml whole milk

2 egg yolks

1–2 tablespoons caster sugar

serves 4

Scrape out the seeds from the vanilla pod and reserve. Put the milk, vanilla seeds and vanilla pod in a pan. Bring to boiling point, then turn off the heat and infuse for 15 minutes. Remove the vanilla pod.

Put the egg yolks and sugar in a bowl and whisk until pale. Pour over the infused milk, mix well and return to the pan. Stir with a wooden spoon over very gentle heat until the custard thickens enough to coat the back of the spoon. Do not allow to overheat or it will curdle.

Use immediately or cover the surface directly with clingfilm, leave to cool, then chill. Reheat very gently before serving.

breads

This loaf has a moist, chewy crumb and a good crunchy crust, and baking it will fill the house with a most wonderful smell. It's a real treat!

old-fashioned cottage loaf

700 g unbleached strong white bread flour

2 teaspoons sea salt

25 g unsalted butter, cubed

15 g fresh yeast*

1 rounded teaspoon honey

450 ml tepid water

1 egg, beaten, to glaze

a large baking sheet, greased

makes 1 large loaf

*To use easy-blend dried yeast, mix one 7-g sachet with the flour and butter mixture, then add the honey and tepid water and mix as in the main recipe.

Mix the flour and salt in a bowl. Add the butter and rub in with your fingertips until the mixture looks like crumbs. Make a well in the centre.

Crumble the yeast into a bowl, add the honey and a quarter of the water, then stir until smooth and creamy. Pour the mixture into the well, then add the remaining water. Gradually work the flour into the liquid to make a slightly firm dough. If the dough feels sticky or soft, work in extra flour, 1 tablespoon at a time. Turn out onto a lightly floured work surface and knead for 10 minutes until the dough feels very pliable and smooth.

Return the dough to the bowl, cover with clingfilm and leave to rise at room temperature until doubled in size, about 1½–2 hours.

Turn out onto a lightly floured work surface and punch down. Cut off one-third of the dough, then gently shape both pieces into balls. Put, well apart, on a well-floured work surface, covered with a sheet of clingfilm, then leave until almost doubled in size, about 45–60 minutes.

Preheat the oven to 230°C (450°F) Gas 8.

Lift the larger ball onto the baking sheet and flatten it slightly. Flatten the smaller ball and set it on top. Push 2 fingers and a thumb joined together down into the middle of the loaf to press both pieces together. Leave for about 5–10 minutes, then glaze with the beaten egg. Using a small sharp knife, score all around the edge of both balls.

Bake for 15 minutes, then reduce the temperature to 200°C (400°F) Gas 6 and bake for 20 minutes, or until the loaf sounds hollow when tapped underneath.

This is the classic Irish soda bread made with bicarbonate of soda as the raising agent rather than yeast. This means that the dough can be baked immediately, rather than having to let it rise as with a yeasted dough. Quick and easy to make.

soda bread

400 g plain wholemeal flour, plus extra to dust

1 teaspoon bicarbonate of soda

1 teaspoon salt

1 teaspoon sugar

300 ml buttermilk

makes 1 small loaf

Preheat the oven to 230°C (450°F) Gas 8.

Put the flour, bicarbonate of soda, salt and sugar into a bowl and mix well. Make a well in the centre, add the buttermilk and gradually work it into the flour to make a soft dough.

Knead on a lightly floured surface for 5 minutes and then shape into a flattened round loaf. Transfer to a greased baking sheet and, using a sharp knife, cut a cross in the top of the dough. Dust with a little extra flour.

Bake for 15 minutes, then reduce the temperature to 200°C (400°F) Gas 6 and bake for a further 30 minutes, or until risen and the loaf sounds hollow when tapped underneath.

Transfer to a wire rack and leave to cool completely.

A quick and simple bread that's perfect for serving alongside a cheese board. This bread goes well with all kinds of cheeses, especially young goats' cheese, Cheddar-style cheeses and creamy blues.

raisin and rosemary bread

250 g strong white flour, plus extra to dust

150 g strong wholemeal flour

100 g rye flour

1½ teaspoons easy-blend dried yeast

1½ teaspoons fine sea salt

1 tablespoon finely chopped fresh rosemary leaves plus 2 extra sprigs for topping

1 tablespoon soft dark brown sugar

310 ml tepid water

2 tablespoons olive oil

110 g raisins

makes 1 medium loaf

Put the white, wholemeal and rye flours in a large bowl and mix. Add the yeast, sea salt and rosemary and stir. Dissolve the sugar in 2 tablespoons of the water. Make a well in the flour and pour in the dissolved sugar and olive oil, followed by the remaining water. Start working the flour into the liquid with a wooden spoon then mix with your hands until all the flour is incorporated.

Turn the dough onto a lightly floured work surface and knead for 5 minutes, or until the dough begins to feel elastic. Flatten the dough and add half the raisins. Fold over and knead for a couple of seconds then repeat with the remaining raisins. Carry on kneading for a further 5 minutes. Put the dough in a large bowl, cover with a slightly damp tea towel and leave for 45–50 minutes, or until doubled in size.

Turn out the dough and punch down. Roll up into a sausage shape and tuck in the ends. Put on a greased baking sheet, make 3 or 4 diagonal cuts in the dough with a sharp knife, cover with the damp tea towel and leave for a further 25 minutes.

Preheat the oven to 200°C (400°F) Gas 6.

Brush the top of the loaf lightly with water and scatter the remaining rosemary leaves on top, pressing them lightly into the dough. Bake for 35–40 minutes, or until the loaf is well browned and sounds hollow when tapped on the base. Leave to cool on a wire rack for at least 45 minutes before serving.

25 g unsalted butter

1 large leek, trimmed and finely chopped, about 150 g prepared weight

a good pinch of dried sage or 1 teaspoon chopped fresh sage (optional)

freshly ground black pepper

230 g unbleached strong white bread flour

230 g strong stoneground wholemeal bread flour

1½ teaspoons sea salt

150 ml tepid milk mixed with 150 ml tepid water

15 g fresh yeast*

140 g Caerphilly cheese

to glaze

3 tablespoons milk mixed with a good pinch of salt

cracked wheat berries or oatmeal, to sprinkle

2 baking sheets, greased

makes 2 round loaves

*To use easy-blend dried yeast, mix one 7-g sachet with the flours and salt, then add the milk and water mixture and continue as in the main recipe.

Bread flavoured with leeks or onions plus cheese and sage is commonly found in Wales and west England.

caerphilly and leek bread

Melt the butter in a frying pan. Add the leek, sage and pepper and cook slowly, stirring occasionally, until softened. Leave to cool until just warm.

Mix the flours and salt in a large bowl, then make a well in the centre. Put the milk-water mixture into a bowl, crumble the yeast over the top and stir until completely dispersed. Pour into the well, then gradually work in the flour to make a soft dough. If the dough feels sticky, work in a little more flour, 1 tablespoon at a time: if the dough feels tough and dry, work in a little more tepid milk or water, 1 tablespoon at a time.

Turn out the dough on a lightly floured work surface and knead for 10 minutes, or until very pliable. Gently work in the leek mixture until thoroughly mixed, then flatten the dough until it is about 2 cm thick. Crumble the cheese onto the dough. Cut the dough into three equal pieces and stack them together, pressing down well. Cut the stack in half, then put one piece on top of the other and press down. Return the dough to the bowl, cover with clingfilm, then leave to rise in a warm place until doubled in size, about 1 hour.

Turn out onto a lightly floured work surface and punch down. Divide into two 14-cm discs. Set on the prepared sheets, then put in a large plastic bag and inflate slightly. Leave to rise as before until almost doubled in size, about 45 minutes. Preheat the oven to 220°C (425°F) Gas 7.

Uncover the loaves and brush lightly with the milk-salt mixture. Sprinkle with cracked wheat berries. Bake for 25 minutes, or until they are golden brown and sound hollow when tapped underneath. Leave to cool slightly on a wire rack. Eat while still warm.

Bread made with a good proportion of cooled mashed potatoes has a wonderful flavour, excellent light texture and lots of nutritional value. Popular with Irish settlers in America, Australia and New Zealand, this bread is well worth adding to your repertoire. Use floury old potatoes in the ratio of four parts flour to one part mashed potato.

potato bread rolls

800 g unbleached strong white bread flour

50 g unsalted butter, cubed

1 tablespoon sea salt

200 g boiled, cooled and mashed potatoes

375 ml tepid milk

15 g fresh yeast*

2 baking sheets, greased

makes 18 rolls

*To use easy-blend dried yeast, mix one 7-g sachet with the flour, then rub in the butter, mix in the salt and potato, and bind to a dough with the milk.

Put the flour in a large mixing bowl, add the butter and rub in with your fingertips until the mixture looks like fine crumbs. Stir in the salt and mashed potatoes.

Put the milk in a jug, crumble the yeast over the top and stir well until dispersed. Pour onto the flour mixture and mix to make a firm dough.

Turn out onto a floured work surface and knead for 10 minutes. Return the dough to the bowl, cover with clingfilm and leave to rise in a warm place until doubled in size, about 1½ hours.

Turn out the risen dough and punch down. Divide the dough into 18 equal pieces. Arrange on the prepared baking sheets, then slip them into 2 large plastic bags and leave to rise as before until doubled in size, about 30 minutes.

Preheat the oven to 220°C (425°F) Gas 7.

Uncover the loaves and bake for 15–20 minutes, or until they sound hollow when tapped underneath. Leave to cool on a wire rack.

Crisp, crumbly Scottish oatcakes have been made for centuries and are still very popular. They are good with soft cheeses or strong Cheddars, or spread with butter and jam or honey. This recipe uses olive oil rather than the traditional lard, as well as fine oatmeal, available from wholefood stores.

oatcakes

220 g fine oatmeal, plus extra for rolling out

½ teaspoon sea salt

2 pinches of baking powder

3 tablespoons olive oil

100 ml boiling water

a 6.5-cm biscuit cutter

several baking sheets, greased

makes about 16 oatcakes

Preheat the oven to 160°C (325°F) Gas 3.

Put the oatmeal, salt, baking powder and olive oil in a food processor. With the motor running, pour in the boiling water through the feed tube. Process until the mixture just comes together. Remove the dough from the processor and put onto a work surface sprinkled with oatmeal. If the dough is very sticky, work in a little extra oatmeal – the dough soon firms up. Roll out the dough to about 4 mm thick, then cut out rounds using the biscuit cutter. Knead the trimmings together, then re-roll and cut out more rounds. Arrange the oatcakes slightly apart on the prepared sheets and bake for about 15 minutes, or until the edges are lightly browned.

Leave to cool on the baking sheets for 2 minutes, then transfer to a wire rack to cool completely.

If the oatcakes become soft, they can be crisped up in the oven (heated as above) for 5 minutes.

variations At the same time as the oatmeal, add either:
• 3 pinches of chilli flakes to make spicy oatcakes
• 4 teaspoons poppy seeds or sesame seeds
• 1 tablespoon fresh thyme leaves

teatime

Often referred to as Gentleman's Relish, there's something quintessentially English about anchovy relish spread on crisp little toasts. These sophisticated bites make a wonderful start to afternoon tea, especially when served with a light, refreshing cup of Earl Grey or Darjeeling. Leftover relish can be stored in the refrigerator for several days.

little toasts with anchovy butter

50 g tinned anchovy fillets, about 8, drained

60 ml milk

60 g unsalted butter

a pinch of cayenne pepper

a pinch of ground nutmeg

a pinch of ground coriander

¼ teaspoon freshly squeezed lemon juice

8 quails' eggs

4 wafer-thin slices of wholemeal bread

2–3 tablespoons chopped fresh flat leaf parsley

freshly ground black pepper

makes 16 toasts

Soak the anchovy fillets in the milk for about 10 minutes.

Drain the anchovy fillets and put them in a food processor with the butter, cayenne pepper, nutmeg, coriander, lemon juice and a good grinding of black pepper. Process until smooth and creamy.

Bring a saucepan of water to the boil, add the quails' eggs, then reduce the heat and simmer for about 4 minutes. Drain, then cover in cold water and leave to cool.

To serve, peel the eggs and cut in half lengthways. Toast the slices of bread until crisp and golden. Cut off and discard the crusts, then cut into quarters. Spread with a thin layer of anchovy relish, top with half a quail's egg and sprinkle with a little parsley. Serve immediately.

Savoury scones filled with cream cheese and peppery watercress, or topped with sweet juicy grapes, make a wonderful alternative to the classic sweet Scones with Clotted Cream and Strawberry Jam (page 203). They are just a few mouthfuls each, so you'll still have plenty of room for a few cakes and fancies.

baby cheese scones

225 g plain flour

4 teaspoons baking powder

a pinch of salt

¼ teaspoon freshly ground black pepper

50 g unsalted butter, chilled and cubed

75 g mature Cheddar cheese, grated

1 egg

100 ml milk

to serve

about 150 g cream cheese

about 40 g watercress or 200 g seedless grapes, halved

a 4-cm biscuit cutter

makes 16 scones

Preheat the oven to 220°C (425°F) Gas 7.

Put the flour, baking powder, salt and pepper in a food processor and pulse to combine. Add the butter and process for about 20 seconds until the mixture resembles fine breadcrumbs. Transfer to a large bowl and stir in 50 g of the cheese, then make a well in the centre of the mixture.

Beat together the egg and milk in another bowl, reserving 1 tablespoon of the mixture in a separate bowl. Pour most of the remaining liquid into the flour mixture and bring together into a soft dough using a fork. If there are still dry crumbs, add a little more of the liquid. Turn out onto a lightly floured surface and knead very briefly, then gently pat or roll out to about 2 cm thick. Cut out rounds with the biscuit cutter, pressing the trimmings together to make more scones.

Arrange the scones on a greased baking sheet, spacing them slightly apart. Brush the tops with the reserved egg and milk mixture and sprinkle over the remaining cheese. Bake for about 10 minutes, or until risen and golden. Transfer to a wire rack and leave to cool.

To serve, split the scones and spread the bottom half with a thick layer of cream cheese, top with watercress, then finish with the scone lid. Alternatively, split the scones, spread each half with cream cheese and top with halved grapes.

These were named after the maids of honour who carried them back to Richmond Palace for King Henry VIII or Queen Elizabeth I – both monarchs, it is said, loved these little cheesecakes made by a local baker. These include a spoonful of best cherry conserve in the base of each – almond and cherry make a great combination. Make these in small, deep tins if you can find them, as the filling seems moister and they look great!

little richmond maids of honour

400 g ready-made sweet shortcrust pastry, at room temperature

8 sprigs of rosemary (optional)

icing sugar, to dust

filling

50 g unsalted butter

75 g caster sugar

finely grated zest and juice of 1 unwaxed lemon

125 g curd or cottage cheese

2 large eggs, beaten

75 ml brandy or cherry brandy

125 g ground almonds

a pinch of salt

about 12 tablespoons cherry conserve

eight 10-cm loose-based tartlet tins

makes 8 maids of honour

Roll out the pastry thinly on a lightly floured work surface and use to line the tartlet tins. Set on a baking sheet and refrigerate for 30 minutes.

Preheat the oven to 180°C (350°F) Gas 4.

Put the butter, sugar and lemon zest in a large bowl and beat until pale and fluffy. Strain the curd into another bowl (do not blend in a food processor, otherwise the texture will be altered), then beat the curd into the butter and sugar mixture. Beat in the eggs, lemon juice and brandy, then gently fold in the ground almonds and a pinch of salt.

Drop a spoonful of cherry conserve in each pastry case, then add the almond filling to about two-thirds full to leave room for rising. Bake for 20–25 minutes, or until risen and golden brown. Remove from the oven and leave to cool slightly. Spear each cheesecake with a sprig of fresh rosemary and serve warm, dusted with icing sugar.

note The cheesecakes may also be made in smaller, deeper tins, but will need a longer cooking time.

400 g ready-made *pâte sucrée* or
sweet shortcrust pastry,
at room temperature

600 ml whole milk

3 fresh (preferably) or dried
bay leaves

6 egg yolks

75 g caster sugar

1 whole nutmeg

*eight 10-cm loose-based tart tins
(or use smaller but deeper tins and
increase the cooking time)*

makes about 8 tarts

There's nothing quite as delicious as a real custard tart.
The nutmeg is the classic flavouring here, but the milk is
also infused with fresh bay leaves to add a mysterious
musky scent to the custard. Fresh bay leaves should be
more widely used in cooking – the flavour is like nutmeg,
but 'greener' and sweeter.

little nutmeg and bay leaf custard tarts

Preheat the oven to 200°C (400°F) Gas 6 and put a baking sheet on the
middle shelf to preheat.

Roll out the pastry thinly on a lightly floured work surface and use to line
the tart tins. Put these on a baking sheet and refrigerate for 30 minutes.

Put the milk and bay leaves in a saucepan and heat until lukewarm. Put
the egg yolks and sugar into a bowl and beat until pale and creamy. Pour
the warmed milk onto the yolks and stir well – do not whisk or you will
get bubbles. Strain into a jug and pour into the tart cases. Grate fresh
nutmeg liberally over the surface of the tartlets.

Put the tart tins on the preheated sheet and bake for 10 minutes.
Reduce the temperature to 180°C (350°F) Gas 4 and bake until set and
just golden – about 10 minutes. Don't overbake as the custard should
be a bit wobbly when the tarts come out of the oven.

Remove from the tins and leave to cool on a wire rack. Serve at room
temperature.

Along with Traditional Christmas Pudding (see page 163), mince pies are also an essential part of British yuletide festivities. To give the pies an extra Christmassy feel, cut the pastry lids into star shapes using a star-shaped cutter, rather than rounds.

mince pies

225 g plain flour

a pinch of salt

115 g butter, chilled and cubed

225 g mincemeat

milk, to glaze

caster sugar, to dust

whipped cream or Brandy Butter (page 163), to serve

a 7.5-cm fluted biscuit cutter

a 6-cm fluted biscuit cutter

a 12-hole muffin tin, greased

makes 12 mince pies

Sift the flour and salt in a bowl and add the butter. Using your fingertips, lightly rub the butter into the flour until the mixture resembles fine breadcrumbs. Gradually add 3–4 tablespoons water, stirring with a blunt knife or a palette knife, until the mixture begins to come together in large lumps. Add a little extra water, if necessary.

Collect the dough together and knead it gently, very briefly, on a lightly floured surface. Wrap in clingfilm and refrigerate for 30 minutes.

Preheat the oven to 190°C (375°F) Gas 5.

Roll out just over half the pastry on a lightly floured surface and stamp out 12 circles of pastry using the larger cutter. Gently press into the muffin tin. Divide the mincemeat evenly between the pastry cases.

Roll out the remaining pastry and stamp out 12 pastry circles using the smaller cutter. Dampen the edges of the pastry circles with water, then place them on top of the mincemeat and pastry in the muffin tin, dampened edges down. Press the edges together to seal. Glaze the tops of the pies with a little milk, then dust with caster sugar. Using a sharp knife, cut a slit in the top of each pie. Bake for 20–25 minutes, or until the pastry is cooked and lightly browned.

Remove from the oven and leave the mince pies in the tin for a couple of minutes, then transfer to a wire rack to cool. Serve warm with whipped cream or Brandy Butter.

Rich, traditional and crumbly, these biscuits were made to contrast with the privations of Lent, and echo the rich (and expensive) flavours of simnel cakes – dried fruit, butter and spices or lemon.

west country easter biscuits

115 g unsalted butter, softened

80 g golden caster sugar

1 egg yolk

the finely grated zest of 1 unwaxed lemon

200 g plain flour

a good pinch of baking powder

a pinch of salt

50 g sultanas

topping

1 egg white, lightly beaten

golden caster sugar, to dust

a 7-cm fluted biscuit cutter

several baking sheets, greased

makes 16 biscuits

Put the butter, sugar and egg yolk in a bowl and beat until light and creamy. Beat in the lemon zest, then add the flour, baking powder, salt and sultanas. Mix with a wooden spoon. Bring the dough together with your hands. Wrap in clingfilm and refrigerate until firm – about 20 minutes. At this point, the dough can be stored in the refrigerator for up to 3 days.

Preheat the oven to 200°C (400°F) Gas 6.

Roll out the dough on a floured work surface to about 5 mm thick. Cut into rounds with the biscuit cutter. Arrange well apart on the prepared baking sheets. Bake for about 10 minutes, or until pale golden and firm.

Remove the sheets from the oven and lightly glaze each biscuit with beaten egg white, then dust with a little sugar. Return to the oven and bake for a further 3–5 minutes, or until the tops are golden and crunchy.

Remove from the oven and leave to cool on the sheets for a minute, then transfer to a wire rack to cool completely.

variation Omit the lemon zest. Add $\frac{1}{2}$ teaspoon ground mixed spice, $\frac{1}{2}$ teaspoon ground cinnamon and a good pinch of grated nutmeg to the flour. Use currants or raisins instead of the sultanas, and add 1 teaspoon finely chopped mixed candied peel if you like.

Parkin is a kind of sticky gingerbread from Yorkshire, made with oatmeal, black treacle and spice. These cookies are made from the same ingredients and have the same flavour and a crunchy texture.

parkin cookies

115 g self-raising flour

115 g fine oatmeal

1 teaspoon ground ginger

½ teaspoon ground allspice

3 tablespoons dark muscovado sugar

85 g unsalted butter

2 tablespoons golden syrup

1 tablespoon black treacle

icing sugar, to dust (optional)

several baking sheets, greased

makes 20 cookies

Preheat the oven to 180°C (350°F) Gas 4.

Put the flour, oatmeal, ginger, allspice and sugar in a large bowl and mix well. Make a hollow in the centre.

Put the butter, golden syrup and treacle in a small saucepan and heat gently until melted.

Pour the mixture into the hollow in the dry ingredients and mix well with a wooden spoon. Using floured hands, take walnut-sized portions of the dough (about a tablespoon) and roll into balls. Set well apart on the prepared baking sheets. Bake for 15 minutes, or until firm.

Leave to cool on the sheets for 2 minutes to firm up, then transfer to a wire rack to cool completely. Serve dusted with icing sugar, if using.

The better the butter you use here, the finer the flavour and texture – a salty, blended butter will make the shortbread heavier so use a good unsalted one. Shortbread can be cut into discs or pressed into a shallow cake tin to make 'petticoat tails'.

scottish shortbread

260 g plain flour

40 g rice flour, ground rice or cornflour

100 g caster sugar, plus extra to dust

200 g unsalted butter, chilled and cubed

a 23-cm sandwich tin, lightly greased, or a 7.5-cm fluted biscuit cutter

several baking sheets, greased

makes about 20 rounds or 12 petticoat tails

Put the plain flour, rice flour and sugar in a food processor. Process until thoroughly mixed. Add the butter and process until everything comes together to make a ball of dough. Carefully remove from the machine.

If making petticoat tails, lightly flour your fingers, then gently press the dough into the sandwich tin to make an even layer. Prick the dough all over with a fork, then gently score into 12 segments using a sharp knife.

If making rounds, roll out the dough on a lightly floured work surface to about 5 mm thick and cut out rounds with the biscuit cutter. Knead the trimmings, then re-roll and cut out more rounds. Put the rounds slightly apart on the prepared baking sheets. Prick all over with a fork.

Preheat the oven to 180°C (350°F) Gas 4.

Refrigerate the shortbread for 15 minutes, then bake for 15–20 minutes for the petticoat tails and 10–12 minutes for the rounds, or until just firm and barely coloured. Dust the shortbread with a little sugar, then leave to cool for 2 minutes. For petticoat tails, cut the segments along the marked lines, then leave until cold before removing from the tin. For the rounds, transfer to a wire rack to cool completely.

These are the stuff of childhood teatimes when you slathered butter on a piping hot crumpet and let the molten butter drip down your chin. They're just as good with jam or honey, and a steaming cup of tea.

crumpets

285 ml milk mixed with 285 ml water

15 g fresh yeast*

450 g plain flour

½ teaspoon bicarbonate of soda

1 teaspoon salt

to serve

unsalted butter

berry jam or honey

2–3 crumpet rings or biscuit cutters

a flat grill-pan or frying pan, preheated and greased

makes 12 crumpets

*To use easy-blend dried yeast, mix one 7-g sachet with the flour and continue as in the main recipe.

Warm the milk and water mixture in a small saucepan. If using fresh yeast, put it into a small bowl with a little of the warm liquid, stir well, then add the remaining milk and water. Sift the flour into a mixing bowl, then stir in the warm yeast mixture.

Cover the bowl with a clean tea towel and leave in a warm place for 1 hour.

Put the bicarbonate of soda and salt into a bowl, add 2 tablespoons water, mix well, then beat it into the mixture. Set aside for a further 45 minutes.

Put the greased crumpet rings on the prepared grill-pan and set over medium heat. When the rings are hot, spoon 2 tablespoons of the batter into each ring – just enough to cover the base. Cook for 4–5 minutes, until the underside is golden, then remove the rings and turn the crumpet over to brown the top.

To serve, toast the crumpets on both sides, smother them with butter and stack on a hot plate. Serve with extra butter and a dish of berry jam or honey. A cup of tea is the traditional accompaniment.

Squidgy and spicy, and dripping with melted butter, nothing quite makes a teatime like hot buttered teacakes. These ones are small, rather than the traditional large ones, so there'll be plenty of room for those other teatime scones and sandwiches.

toasted teacakes

225 g strong white bread flour

½ teaspoon salt

1 teaspoon easy-blend dried yeast

1½ tablespoons soft brown sugar

¼ teaspoon freshly grated nutmeg

50 g mixed dried fruits

3 ready-to-eat dried apricots, chopped

40 g butter

120 ml milk, plus extra to glaze

2 baking sheets, greased

makes 8 teacakes

Combine the flour, salt, yeast, sugar and nutmeg in a bowl, then sift into a larger bowl. Stir in the dried fruits, then make a well in the centre.

Melt the butter in a small saucepan, then add the milk and heat until lukewarm. Pour into the flour mixture, gradually working it in to make a soft dough. Turn out onto a lightly floured surface and knead for about 5 minutes, or until smooth and elastic. Transfer to a bowl, wrap in a plastic bag and leave to rise in a warm place for about 1 hour, or until doubled in size.

Turn the dough out onto a lightly floured work surface, punch down and divide into 8 equal pieces. Shape each one into a disc and arrange on the prepared baking sheets, spacing them slightly apart. Wrap the baking sheets in plastic bags and leave to rise as above for about 45 minutes, or until doubled in size.

Preheat the oven to 200°C (400°F) Gas 6.

Brush the teacakes with milk, then bake for about 15 minutes, or until risen and golden, and they sound hollow when tapped. Transfer to a wire rack to cool. To serve, cut the teacakes in half and toast, then spread generously with butter.

Traditionally served with clotted cream and rich, fruity jam, these classic scones are a must for the tea table. In fact, there is nothing that symbolizes British afternoon tea quite as well as a scone. Originally made in Devon and Cornwall, clotted cream is formed by gently heating milk to produce a really rich, thick cream.

scones *with clotted cream and strawberry jam*

225 g self-raising flour

1 teaspoon baking powder

2 tablespoons caster sugar

50 g unsalted butter, chilled and cubed

1 egg

75 ml milk

to serve

clotted cream

good-quality strawberry jam

a 4-cm or 5-cm biscuit cutter

makes 10–12 scones

Preheat the oven to 220°C (425°F) Gas 7.

Put the flour, baking powder and sugar in a food processor and pulse to combine. Add the butter and process for about 20 seconds until the mixture resembles fine breadcrumbs. Transfer to a large bowl and make a well in the centre.

Beat together the egg and milk in another bowl, reserving 1 tablespoon of the mixture in a separate bowl. Pour most of the remaining liquid into the flour mixture and bring together into a soft dough using a fork. If there are still dry crumbs, add a little more of the liquid. Turn out onto a lightly floured surface and knead briefly until smooth. Work in a little more flour if the mixture is sticky. Gently pat or roll out the dough to about 2.5 cm thick and cut out rounds using the biscuit cutter, pressing the trimmings together to make more scones.

Arrange the scones on a greased baking sheet, spacing them slightly apart, and glaze the tops with the reserved egg and milk mixture. Bake for about 8 minutes, or until risen and golden. Transfer to a wire rack to cool slightly. Serve warm with clotted cream and strawberry jam.

These fruity, spiced, spiralled buns have been a traditional English treat since the eighteenth century. They were first made and sold by the celebrated Chelsea Bun House in Chelsea, west London.

baby chelsea buns

450 g strong white bread flour

1 teaspoon salt

50 g caster sugar

a 7-g sachet of easy-blend dried yeast

90 g butter, melted

150 ml milk

2 eggs, beaten

80 g soft brown sugar

1 teaspoon ground cinnamon

75 g sultanas

25 g currants

50 g ready-to-eat dried apricots, chopped

clear honey, to glaze

a 20-cm square cake tin, greased

makes 16 buns

Sift the flour, salt, caster sugar and yeast in a large bowl and make a well in the centre. Put 60 g of the butter in a small saucepan with the milk and heat until lukewarm. Remove from the heat, stir in the beaten eggs, then pour into the flour mixture, gradually working it in to make a soft dough. Turn out onto a lightly floured surface and knead for 5–10 minutes until smooth and elastic. Return to the bowl, wrap in a plastic bag and leave to rise in a warm place for about 1 hour, or until doubled in size.

Punch down the dough, then divide into 4 equal pieces. Roll out each piece on a lightly floured surface to 12 x 20 cm. Combine the brown sugar, cinnamon and dried fruits in a bowl and toss to mix. Pour the remaining melted butter over the dough, brushing it towards the edges to cover evenly. Sprinkle the fruit mixture on top and roll up tightly from the long edge to make 4 rolls.

Slice each roll into 4 whirls and arrange them in the prepared cake tin so that they are barely touching. Wrap in a plastic bag and leave to rise in a warm place for about 30 minutes, or until doubled in size.

Preheat the oven to 200°C (400°F) Gas 6.

Take the cake tin out of the plastic bag and bake for 20 minutes, or until golden. Glaze the buns with honey and bake for a further 5 minutes. Leave to cool in the tin for about 10 minutes, then turn out onto a wire rack and leave to cool completely. Pull the buns apart to serve.

450 g unbleached strong white bread flour

50 g stoneground wholemeal bread flour

50 g caster sugar

1 teaspoon sea salt

1 teaspoon ground mixed spice

½ teaspoon freshly grated nutmeg

50 g unsalted butter, cubed

60 g currants

25 g sultanas

25 g finely chopped mixed peel

15 g fresh yeast

250 ml tepid milk

1 large egg, beaten

pastry cross

60 g plain flour

30 g unsalted butter, diced

2 teaspoons caster sugar

4 tablespoons milk mixed with 3 tablespoons caster sugar, to glaze

2 baking sheets, greased

makes 12 buns

Traditionally marked with a cross, these rich spicy fruit buns are eaten on Good Friday.

extra spicy hot cross buns

Put the flours, sugar, salt and spices in a large bowl and mix well. Add the butter and rub into the flour using your fingertips until the mixture resembles fine crumbs. Mix in the dried fruit and mixed peel, then make a well in the centre of the mixture.

Crumble the yeast into a small bowl, pour in about half the milk and stir until completely dispersed. Add to the well in the flour with the rest of the milk and the egg. Gradually draw in the flour to make a soft but not sticky dough. Work in a little extra flour or milk if necessary.

Turn out the dough onto a lightly floured work surface and knead for 10 minutes. Return the dough to the bowl, then cover with clingfilm. Leave to rise in a warm place until doubled in size, about 1½ hours.

Turn the dough out onto a lightly floured work surface, then punch down. Divide into 12 neat balls and set well apart on the prepared baking sheets. Slip the sheets into large plastic bags, inflate slightly and leave to rise as before until doubled in size, 45–60 minutes. Meanwhile, preheat the oven to 200°C (400°F) Gas 6.

To make the pastry cross, put the flour, butter and sugar in a bowl and rub the butter into the flour with your fingertips until you get coarse crumbs. Stir in 1–2 tablespoons cold water to make a firm dough. Roll the dough out thinly.

Uncover the risen buns, brush the pastry strips with a little water, then stick in a cross on top of the buns. Bake for 15–20 minutes, or until golden brown. Heat the milk-sugar glaze in a pan until dissolved, then boil for 1 minute. Glaze the buns as soon as they come out of the oven.

Rich and sweetly spiced, this teabread is known as Bara Brith in Wales, a name which means 'speckled bread'. It was traditionally made with leftover dough at the end of the day when the cook 'speckled' the dough with currants. Mixed spice is often called pudding spice or sweet spice and reflects the centuries-long British love of spices.

welsh teabread

275 g mixed dried fruit, such as sultanas, raisins and citrus peel

325 ml hot black tea

325 g plain flour

2 teaspoons baking powder

1¼–1½ teaspoons mixed spice

100 g unsalted butter, melted

150 g golden caster sugar or soft brown sugar

½–1 teaspoon dark treacle, to colour

1 egg, beaten

a 900-g loaf tin, lined with greaseproof paper

makes 1 large teabread

Put the dried fruit in a bowl, add the hot tea and leave to soak for at least 30 minutes. Drain the fruit and reserve the tea.

Preheat the oven to 160°C (325°F) Gas 3.

Put the flour, baking powder and mixed spice in a bowl and mix well. Put the melted butter into a separate bowl, add the reserved tea, sugar and treacle and mix well. Add the beaten egg and fruit and mix again.

Pour the fruit mixture gradually into the flour and mix well into a sloppy dough. Pour the dough into the prepared loaf tin and bake on the middle shelf of the oven for about 1 hour 15 minutes, or until a skewer inserted into the centre comes out clean and the top is evenly brown. It should be dark and moist – be careful towards the end of baking as the top can scorch easily.

Remove from the oven and transfer to a wire rack. Leave to cool a little before serving. Cut thick slices, spread them with butter, then serve with a cup of tea – a perfect afternoon interlude.

225 g unsalted butter,
at room temperature

225 g golden caster sugar

4 large eggs, at room temperature,
lightly beaten

1 teaspoon vanilla extract

225 g self-raising flour

75 g dark chocolate, chopped

1 tablespoon cocoa powder

75 g white chocolate, chopped

*a 900-g loaf tin,
greased and base-lined*

makes 1 large loaf cake

The classic English pound cake recipe uses equal weights of butter, flour, sugar and eggs. It's very easy to turn the basic sponge mixture into an impressive, richly flavoured marbled loaf. Serve thick slices with a cup of tea or coffee and watch the cake disappear in no time.

black and white chocolate marble loaf cake

Preheat the oven to 180°C (350°F) Gas 4.

Put the butter into a large mixing bowl and beat until very creamy. Beat in the sugar and continue beating for about 2 minutes, or until the mixture is lighter in colour and consistency. Gradually beat in the eggs, then the vanilla extract. Sift in the flour and fold in with a metal spoon.

Spoon half the cake mixture into another mixing bowl. Put the dark chocolate in a heatproof bowl set over a pan of simmering water and melt gently (do not let the base of the bowl touch the water). Remove from the heat and leave to cool. Sift the cocoa onto one portion of cake mixture, add the dark chocolate, then, using a metal spoon, fold in until evenly mixed.

Melt the white chocolate as above. When cool, fold into the remaining portion of cake mixture using a clean metal spoon.

Spoon both cake mixtures into the prepared tin, using each mixture alternately. Draw a knife through the mixtures and swirl together.

Bake for about 1¼ hours, or until a skewer inserted in the centre comes out clean. Turn out onto a wire rack, remove the lining and leave to cool.

Named after Queen Victoria, this classic cake filled with cream and fresh fruit makes a wonderful centrepiece for a traditional afternoon tea. Make it in summer when strawberries are in season and at their best.

victoria sandwich
with strawberries and cream

180 g butter, at room temperature

180 g caster sugar

3 eggs

180 g self-raising flour

3½ tablespoons good-quality strawberry jam

140 g strawberries, hulled and halved or quartered, depending on size

120 ml whipping cream

icing sugar, to dust

two 20-cm sandwich tins, greased and base-lined with greaseproof paper

serves 6–8

Preheat the oven to 180°C (350°F) Gas 4.

Beat together the butter and caster sugar in a large bowl until pale and fluffy. Beat in the eggs one at a time. Sift the flour into the mixture and fold in until thoroughly combined.

Spoon the cake mixture into the prepared tins and spread out evenly using the back of the spoon. Bake for 20–25 minutes, or until golden brown and the sponge springs back when pressed gently with the tips of your fingers. Turn out the cakes onto a wire rack, gently peel off the lining paper and leave to cool completely.

To serve, slice a thin slither off the top of one of the cakes to create a flat surface. Spread the strawberry jam on top and top with the strawberries. Whip the cream until it stands in soft peaks, then spread on top of the strawberries. Top with the second cake, press down gently and dust with icing sugar.

Picture a traditional afternoon tea at an English tea parlour and there is bound to be a luscious coffee cake topped with crisp brown walnuts. An old favourite that never fails to please.

coffee and walnut cake

180 g butter, at room temperature

180 g caster sugar

3 eggs

180 g self-raising flour

60 g walnut pieces

2 teaspoons instant coffee, dissolved in 1 tablespoon boiling water

walnut halves, to decorate

icing

2 tablespoons single cream

2 teaspoons instant coffee

90 g butter, at room temperature

180 g icing sugar

two 20-cm sandwich tins, greased and base-lined with greaseproof paper

serves 6–8

Preheat the oven to 180°C (350°F) Gas 4.

Beat together the butter and sugar in a large bowl until pale and fluffy, then beat in the eggs one at a time. Sift the flour into the butter mixture and fold in, then fold in the nuts and dissolved coffee. Divide among the prepared sandwich tins and spread out evenly. Bake for 20–25 minutes, or until golden and the sponge springs back when pressed gently with the tips of your fingers. Turn the cakes out onto a wire rack, carefully peel off the lining paper and leave to cool completely.

To make the icing, warm the cream and coffee in a small saucepan, stirring until the coffee has dissolved. Pour into a bowl, add the butter and sift the icing sugar into the mixture. Beat together until smooth and creamy.

To serve, slice a thin slither off the top of one of the cakes to create a flat surface. Spread with slightly less than half of the icing, then place the second cake on top. Spread the remaining icing on top and decorate with walnut halves.

If you can make muffins, you can make this cake. It is really a rich chocolate chip muffin recipe, so just measure and mix. The icing is a simple butter icing made with cocoa.

triple chocolate layer cake

450 g self-raising flour

60 g cocoa powder

a good pinch of salt

400 g caster sugar

225 ml sunflower oil

2 large eggs, beaten

225 ml milk

1 teaspoon vanilla extract

150 g dark chocolate, chopped

icing

125 g unsalted butter, softened

330 g icing sugar

6 tablespoons cocoa powder

4 tablespoons milk

½ teaspoon vanilla extract

three 20-cm sandwich tins

serves 8

Preheat the oven to 180°C (350°F) Gas 4. Grease the sandwich tins and base-line with greaseproof paper.

Sift the flour, cocoa, salt and sugar into a large bowl, and make a well in the centre. Pour the oil, beaten eggs, milk and vanilla extract into the well, and mix gradually with a wooden spoon. Add the chopped chocolate and stir well. Divide the mixture between the 3 prepared tins.

Bake for 20–25 minutes, or until a skewer inserted in the centre comes out clean. Leave to cool in the tins for 5 minutes, then carefully turn out onto a wire rack to cool completely.

To make the icing, put the butter in a bowl and beat until very creamy. Gradually beat in the icing sugar, cocoa, milk and vanilla extract to make a thick, smooth icing.

When the cakes are completely cold, use the icing to layer them. Spread about one-sixth of the icing on the top of one cake. Gently set a second cake on top and spread with another one-sixth of the icing. Top with the last cake, then coat the top and sides with the rest of the icing. Decorate with extra chopped chocolate, if desired.

Make this sensational summer drink when lemons are ripe and plentiful. Leave the lemons on a warm windowsill for a few days to sweeten them up and develop their flavour. You can make this a day or two ahead. It must be served as cold as possible.

real old-fashioned lemonade

3 unwaxed lemons, scrubbed in warm water

200 g sugar

1 litre boiling water

sprigs of mint or lemon balm (optional)

serves 2–4

Using a potato peeler, remove the yellow zest from the lemons in long strips, avoiding any bitter white pith. Put it in a large heatproof jug, add the sugar and pour over the boiling water. Stir well to dissolve the sugar, cover and leave to cool completely.

Squeeze the juice from the lemons, strain and set aside. When the lemon-scented water is cold, stir in the lemon juice and strain into a jug. Chill well and serve poured over ice, with a sprig of mint or lemon balm, if using.

2 tablespoons pearl barley

1.5 litres boiling water

grated zest and juice of 1 large unwaxed lemon

2 teaspoons sugar

a curl of lemon zest

ice, to serve

serves 2–4

In Victorian times, kitchen maids would boil up the lemon and barley, strain it through muslin, leave it to cool, then struggle to find a way to chill it. Thank goodness for ice!

lemon barley water

Put the barley and water in a saucepan and simmer for 30 minutes. Strain into a cafetière, then stir in the sugar, lemon zest and juice. Leave to cool, plunge, chill, then serve over ice with a curl of lemon zest.

preserves

Chutney, a cherished sweet and spicy condiment on the British table, is an Anglo-Indian remnant from the days of the East India Company and the Raj. Homemade versions have always been popular in England – an aspect of the national taste for jams and pickles to serve with bread, cheese and cold meats. They have acquired a distinctively British flavour, different from their originals in India.

plum chutney

800 g plums, about 14, stoned and chopped

225 g raisins

1 large onion, chopped

½ teaspoon salt

150 ml cider vinegar

1½ teaspoons coriander seeds, 1 teaspoon allspice berries, 10 cloves, ¼ teaspoon black peppercorns and ¾ teaspoon mustard seeds, all in a spice ball or tied up in muslin

½ teaspoon ground ginger

a good pinch of freshly grated nutmeg

140 g sugar or brown sugar

two sterilized 500-ml jars with non-metal lids (see page 4)

two wax discs

makes 800 ml chutney

Put the plums, raisins, onion and salt into a stainless steel (not copper) preserving pan or heavy-based saucepan and add the vinegar. Stir, then add the spice ball or bag of pickling spices. Bring to the boil, reduce the heat and simmer gently for about 40 minutes, stirring occasionally. Be careful not to scorch the chutney as it cooks and thickens.

Add the ginger, nutmeg and sugar and mix well. Keep a close eye on the chutney and cook for another 10–15 minutes, stirring regularly to make sure it doesn't burn. It should be dark and tangy yet sweet and thick. As it cools and sets, it will become thicker still.

Remove the spice ball or bag of pickling spices and pour the chutney into the sterilized jars while still hot. Line the lids with wax paper and seal at once.

There are many varieties of pumpkin and this recipe can be used to preserve all of them. Make sure that the flesh is firm and not stringy, or it will spoil the finished texture of the chutney. You can also use other vegetables such as marrow, courgettes, aubergines, unripe melons and green tomatoes to make this recipe. Serve with a ploughman's lunch, scrambled eggs or cold meats.

pumpkin and red tomato chutney

400 g peeled and deseeded firm pumpkin or butternut squash flesh, cut into 1-cm cubes

200 g ripe tomatoes, skinned, deseeded and chopped

200 g onions, chopped

25 g sultanas

250 g demerara sugar

1 teaspoon salt

3 cm fresh ginger, peeled and finely chopped

1 garlic clove, peeled and finely chopped

a little freshly grated nutmeg

200 ml malt vinegar, plus 100 ml extra

a sterilized 500-g jar with lid or cover (see page 4)

a waxed paper disc

makes 500 g chutney

Put the pumpkin, tomatoes, onions, sultanas, sugar, salt, ginger, garlic, nutmeg and the 200 ml vinegar in a saucepan and bring slowly to the boil. Simmer for 1 hour, stirring from time to time. The chutney should look dark, dense and rich. Top up with extra vinegar if the chutney dries out too much while cooking.

Transfer to the sterilized jar, cover the surface of the chutney with a waxed disc and seal at once. Label when cool and store for 1–6 months in a cool, dark cupboard before opening.

Like the Pumpkin and Red Tomato Chutney on page 224, these pickled onions are perfect with a ploughman's lunch, or simply with a flavoursome cheese.

pickled onions

60 g salt

500 g shallots or pickling onions

spiced vinegar

8 mixed peppercorns

4 whole cloves

1 cm cinnamon stick

1 cm fresh ginger

400 ml malt vinegar

a sterilized 500-g jar with lid (see page 4)

a waxed paper disc or greaseproof paper

makes 500 g pickled onions

Put the salt in a saucepan with 600 ml water. Bring to the boil, remove from the heat and leave to cool.

Put the shallots in a large bowl, pour boiling water over them and leave for a few minutes. Drain and peel.

Put the shallots in a bowl, add the cooled brine and leave for 24 hours. After this time, drain, rinse in cold water and dry carefully.

To make the spiced vinegar, put the peppercorns, cloves, cinnamon and ginger in a small saucepan, add the vinegar, cover and bring to the boil over low heat. Turn off the heat, leave to cool, then strain.

Pack the onions into the sterilized jar, pushing them down with the handle of a wooden spoon. Top up with the cooled spiced vinegar.

Tap the sides to remove any air bubbles or slide a thin knife blade down the inside of the jar to release them.

Cover with a waxed paper disc or greaseproof paper, seal the jar and store in a cool, dark cupboard until required. Wait at least 3 months before serving.

Marmalade epitomizes an English breakfast. The beauty of this particular marmalade is that it can be made in small quantities at any time of the year, not just when Sevilles are in season.

chunky lemon, lime and grapefruit marmalade

1 unwaxed lemon

1 small unwaxed pink grapefruit

1 unwaxed lime

1 kg sugar

freshly squeezed juice of ½ lemon

three 250-g sterilized jam jars with lids or covers (see page 4)

waxed paper discs

makes 500–750 g marmalade

Scrub the fruit and prise out any stalk ends. Put in a pan and cover with 500 ml water. Set over low heat and cook until tender – 1½–2 hours. The fruit is ready when it 'collapses'.

Transfer the fruit to a chopping board and leave until cool enough to handle. Cut in half, scrape out all the flesh and pips and add to the pan of water. Bring to the boil and simmer for 5 minutes. Cut the zest into strips, or put it in a blender and blend until chunky. Strain the water from the pips and flesh and return it to the pan, adding the chopped zest and the lemon juice. Discard the pips and debris.

Add the sugar to the pan and bring slowly to simmering point, stirring until the sugar has dissolved. The sugar content is high, so this will take quite a long time. When the marmalade has become translucent, you will know the sugar has dissolved and you can increase the heat. Bring to the boil and boil rapidly until setting point is reached – 5–10 minutes.

Take the pan off the heat and test for set (see page 4). If the marmalade is not ready, put the pan back on the heat to boil for a few more minutes and test again. When setting point has been reached, return to simmering point, then turn off the heat. Skim with a perforated skimmer, stir well and leave to stand for 30 minutes. Stir and ladle into the sterilized jars, seal with waxed paper discs and cover with a lid. Leave to cool, label and store in a cool, dark cupboard until needed.

Strawberry and raspberry jam – delicious on scones, crumpets and toast – but super easy and quick to make.

strawberry jam

500 g fresh ripe strawberries, hulled and quartered

350 g sugar with added pectin (sometimes known as 'jam sugar')

two 500-g sterilized jam jars with lids or covers (see page 4)

makes 1½ pots, 500 g each

Put the strawberries in a large bowl with a splash of water. Cover and microwave on FULL for 2 minutes. Carefully uncover and stir in the sugar. Re-cover and cook on FULL for another 2 minutes.

Uncover and stir well to dissolve the sugar. Replace in the microwave uncovered and cook on FULL for 8 minutes.

Test by dropping a teaspoon onto a chilled saucer and chilling in the refrigerator for 10 minutes. If it has set, pour the jam into clean dry jars and cover. If not, microwave for 4 more minutes, then try the test again. Pour into the sterilized jars and seal. After opening, the jam will keep in the refrigerator for up to 2 weeks.

freezer raspberry jam

750 g fresh raspberries

1 kg sugar with added pectin (sometimes known as 'jam sugar')

2 tablespoons freshly squeezed lemon juice

two 500-g sterilized jam jars with lids or covers (see page 4)

makes 2 pots, 500 g each

Tip the raspberries into a bowl and crush a bit with a potato masher. Stir in the jam sugar and lemon juice. Cover with clingfilm and heat on MEDIUM in the microwave for about 5 minutes or until warmed through.

Uncover and stir gently to dissolve the sugar, then leave to stand overnight. Alternatively, heat in a saucepan until the sugar has dissolved.

The next day, pot up into freezer containers and freeze – keep one pot in the refrigerator for breakfast tomorrow. After removing from the freezer, store the jam in the refrigerator. Thaw before using.

If you have space for a small tree in your garden, it's worth planting a crab-apple. You will have pretty blossom in spring and jewel-like miniature apples in the late summer to early autumn. Use them to make this stunning pink jelly to serve with roast pork, poultry and game.

crab-apple jelly

1.5 kg crab-apples

1 unwaxed lemon

sugar or preserving sugar
(see method)

a jelly bag or muslin

*two or three sterilized 250-g jam
jars with lids or covers (see page 4)*

waxed paper discs

makes 500–750 g

Sort the crab-apples, discarding any that are badly bruised or marked and any leaves that are still attached. Wash the fruit, cut them in half and put in a large saucepan. Fill the pan with water to just under the level of the fruit. Peel the zest thinly from the lemon and add this and the peeled lemon to the pan. Part-cover with a lid, bring slowly to the boil and simmer for 1 hour. Transfer to a jelly bag or muslin suspended over a large bowl and leave to drip all night.

Measure the juice into a clean preserving pan and, for every 600 ml of juice, add 450 g sugar. Set over low heat and bring to simmering point, dissolving the sugar, stirring all the while. When it has dissolved, increase the heat and boil hard for 5–10 minutes until setting point is reached.

Take the pan off the heat and test for set (see page 4). If the jelly is not ready, put the pan back on the heat to boil for a few more minutes and test again. When setting point has been reached, return to simmering point, then turn off the heat. Skim with a perforated skimmer, stir and ladle into the sterilized jars. Seal with waxed paper discs and cover with a lid. Leave to cool, label and store in a cool, dark cupboard until needed.

This is a quintessentially British preserve, tart with lemon yet sweet and buttery at the same time. It is delicious on toast or on freshly made scones or bread and also an excellent filling for tarts, sponge cakes or meringues. Small jars make a great gift. It is very easy to make so long as you stir it very frequently as it cooks and keep the heat low so that the water in the pan barely bubbles.

lemon curd

2 large unwaxed lemons

125 g unsalted butter, cut into cubes

180 g caster sugar

3 eggs, beaten

two 225-g sterilized jam jars with lids or covers (see page 4)

makes 2 small jars, 225 g each

Finely grate the zest from the lemons into a heatproof bowl. Squeeze the juice and add that to the bowl with the butter and sugar.

Place the bowl over a pan of just-simmering water, making sure the water doesn't touch the base of the bowl. Stir until the butter melts, add the eggs and, using a wooden spoon, stir for 10–15 minutes until the mixture thickens noticeably and takes on a translucent look.

For a very smooth preserve, strain the curd through a fine sieve into a measuring jug, then pot it into the sterilized jars. Cover with clingfilm or greaseproof paper when cold. It will keep for 15 days in the refrigerator.

index